Your Trav
To Cooking
For A Good Cause

Date of Publication
Volume I - 2001

Published by:
The Charity Appeal's Liaison Office ~ Velindre Hospital
Whitchurch, Cardiff
CF14 2TL
Tel: 029 - 20 - 316211
Fax: 029 - 20 - 522694
(E Mail Appeals.dept@Velindre-tr.Wales.NHS.UK)

Printed by:
ProPrint
Riverside Cottage
Great North Road
Stibbington
Peterborough PE8 6LR

ISBN: 0 9539432 0 8

CONTENTS

ACKNOWLEDGEMENTS

The Charity Appeal's staff at Velindre Hospital confirm their gratitude for the willing support given by the folk who have helped with the publication of our recipe book. Many could be named but perhaps the following are worthy of a special mention!

Fern Britton for her kindness in adding her patronage to this rather exciting venture.

ASDA Newport for their kindness in helping with sales and distribution.

Carolyn Smith (Charity Appeal's Fund-raiser) for her tireless efforts in covering all aspects of compilation and meeting printing deadlines.

Our recipe contributors for their kindness in supplying a very varied content!

ProPrint for their first class printing service ~ and ~

Most importantly of all, *you for your kindness in buying what we hope will prove useful and enjoyable!*

Great care has been taken in the preparation of the content of the recipe book, and no responsibility can be accepted by the publisher for errors or omissions!

FOREWORD

By Miss Fern Britton

This little book has a big mission. While you enjoy reading and cooking the recipes within its pages, the money you handed over for it, is hard at work raising much needed cash for the patients who are treated so wonderfully at the Velindre Hospital, Cardiff. This little book is a life saver and so are you.

Thank you!

love Fern

1

**Julie Smith and Carolyn Smith (Charity Staff) with
Charity Shop Voluntary Workers**

JOHN BURNETT
Appeals Co-ordinator, Velindre Hospital Charity,
Velindre NHS Trust

The Velindre Appeal has, as it's aim, the provision of facilities to further the quality of care and research carried out at Velindre Hospital which is one of the main Cancer Treatment Centres in the United Kingdom. The Appeal addresses itself to clinical and research priorities as identified by the hospital clinicians, and in recent years almost £3m has been raised for patient support at the hospital!

There is little doubt that without charity donation income, care and research at Wales' main centre would be quite significantly hampered, and it is pleasing to report that *every penny* of the revenue raised from the sale of this charity recipe book will be allocated against what are considered essential developments.

Our first charity recipe book was published in conjunction with Marks and Spencer in 1995, and it is hoped that his second venture will receive as much enthusiasm as the first issue! Thank you for your support. I sincerely hope you will find the recipes and other information interesting and useful.

Yours sincerely

Mr Roy Noble - BBC Radio and TV Presenter, one of Velindre's Appeal Patrons, officiating at the opening of Velindre's new Chemotherapy Treatment Centre, built at a cost of almost £1m and raised from charity donations.

Guide To Good Cooking

Throughout the book you will find a variety of weights and measures, so just in case you prefer grammes to ounces, or vice versa, below is a conversion table as an aid.

Oven Temperatures

Mark

1	275F	140C
2	300	150
3	325	170
4	350	180
5	375	190
6	400	200
7	425	220
8	450	230
9	475	240

Weights

½oz	10g
1	25
1½	40
2	50
2½	60
3	75
4	110
4½	125
5	150
6	175
7	200
8	225
9	250
10	275
12	350
1lb	450
1½	700
2	900

Volume

2fl oz	55ml
3	75
5 (¼ Pint)	150
½ Pint	275
¾	425
1	570
1¾	Litre

BUCKETS OF CASH: Jenny Powell, Asda
customer services manager, and John Burnett,
appeals co-ordinator for the Velindre Hospital,
Cardiff, celebrate with Asda staff who raised
£10,000 during 2000.

NOTES

**Stan Stennett (Velindre Appeal Patron) signing
the first charity recipe book published by
Marks & Spencer on behalf of Velindre and
Cancer Research Wales.**

CELEBRITY CHEFS

PHIL VICKERY

Phil Vickery was born in Folkestone, Kent and trained in the Lake District. His first stints as a chef were at Gravity Manor in West Sussex and at Ian McAndrew's Restaurant 74 in Canterbury. From 1990 to 1999 he was at the Castle Hotel in Taunton, one of the best restaurants in Britain, eventually becoming a director and head chef. Phil won the British 'Meat Chef of the Year' Award in 1998; his other professional accolades include earning a Michelin star for three successive years, winning the Egon Ronay *'Dessert of the Year'* category in 1995, and having the Castle named *'Restaurant of the Year'* in 1994. He is well-known for his regular appearances on *Ready, Steady, Cook, Masterchef* and *Who'll Do The Pudding?*

Phil is one of Britain's most highly regarded exciting, young cooks. He is a passionate advocate of unpretentious, honest and robust cooking that will appeal to both men and women. He is particularly famed for his supremely delicious puddings and his 'boozy food'.

Sautéed Peaches With Marscapone, Pistachios And Vanilla Syrup

Serves 6

Ingredients
6 *ripe* peaches, 2 pints of sugar syrup
2 vanilla pods ~ split and seeds removed
2oz peeled pistachios
1 x 8oz carton of good quality Marscapone
A little unsalted butter

Method
Bring the syrup to the boil and drop in the peaches. Remove from the heat, cover with greaseproof paper and a plate and leave to cool.

When cool, take the peaches out carefully and remove the skins.

Cut in half lengthways and remove the stone.

Place on a clean tea towel.

Strain 8fl oz of the peach syrup back into the saucepan and add the vanilla pods and bring back to the boil again and then leave to cool.

To finish the dish, place some butter into a frying pan and heat until just starting to brown.

Add the peach halves and sauté until a nice colour is taken.

Turn over and add the pistachios and some vanilla syrup.

This will boil and reduce almost straight away. Thicken with a touch more butter.

Put the peach halves in a bowl, top with the syrup and finish with Marscapone.

Items from the first Velindre/Cancer Research Wales Celebrity Auction.

KEVIN WOODFORD

Take a vibrant personality, excellent communication skills plus a pinch of cheeky charm and you have the recipe for Kevin Woodford's success. Currently hosting BBC1's live topical magazine programme *The Heaven and Earth Show* in which Kevin tackles contentious current social issues along with the light-hearted topical subjects. The show has proved to be a ratings success.

Kevin first hit our television screens as a regular contributor on ITV's top-rated *This Morning* programme. The BBC tempted Kevin to join them as a regular performer on *Ready Steady Cook* and a main presenter on *Can't Cook, Won't Cook* which was voted 'Best Day Time Television Progamme' at The National Television Awards.

Away from the kitchen, he has reported for 4 years from around the world for the BBC's *Holiday* programme and co-presented its seasonal counterpart *Summer Holiday*. His success on these programmes brought a 'Holiday Special' in which he caused a sensation taking on the role of a cruise ship 'Entertainment's Officer' an ideal which spawned the BBC series *Fasten Your Seat Belts*. Kevin showed he had what it takes to be a Concierge at one of the world's top hotels in Hong Kong, a Yellow Taxi Cab Driver in bustling New York and A Deck Hand on a Caribbean Rigger Ship, which included climbing the rigging to the crow's nest (not the easiest task when you have a lifetime fear of heights).

Kevin is fairly unique in that he is able to bring warmth to any situation, which makes him equally at home with programmes as diverse as light entertainment, current affairs and news. He is a graduate in Management, a skilled communicator and has many successful publications. His current major publication accompanies his recent BBC evening series, a 'humorous travel cookalogue' ~ *Big Kevin, Little Kevin,* which created great excitement amongst the critics.

Kevin's celebrity status has brought him invites to appear on such network programmes as *A Day at the Pictures with Kevin Woodford* (Sky), *The National Lottery Show, Noel's House Party, Bob Monkhouse's Birthday Special, All Over The Shop* (BBC), *Win, Lose or Draw* (ITV), *Ian Wright's Hidden Talent Show* (ITV), to name but a few!

His professionalism and wicked sense of humour means Kevin is fast becoming one of the most sought after presenters on television and in the corporate market.

Hot Raspberry And Chocolate Pudding
With A White Chocolate Sauce And Summer Fruit Compote

This is one of the sexiest puddings around, but be sure to adhere to the cooking times. The pudding should be firm on the outside yet still a little runny on the inside.

Serves 6

For the chocolate pudding:
90g (3½oz) unsalted butter
90g (3½oz) good quality dark chocolate, chopped into small pieces
3 large eggs
3 large egg yolks
75g (3oz) Castor sugar
15g (½oz) plain flour
18 raspberries
icing sugar, to dust
6 small sprigs of mint, to decorate

For the white chocolate sauce:
4 large egg yolks
40g (1½oz) Castor sugar
450ml (¾ pint) milk
40g (1½oz) good quality white chocolate, chopped into small pieces

For the compote of summer fruits:
50g (2oz) strawberries, quartered
50g (2oz) raspberries
25g (1oz) blackcurrants
1tblsp lavender honey

Method

Prepare the white chocolate sauce; in a bowl, whisk the egg yolks and sugar together until light and fluffy. Heat the milk until it boils and pour slowly onto the egg and sugar mixture, stirring to ensure that it is incorporated. Transfer the mixture back into the pan and heat gently, stirring with a wooden spoon, until the mixture gains enough body to coat the back of the spoon. Add the white chocolate pieces to the sauce and mix thoroughly. Remove the sauce from the heat, allow to cool and chill until ready to serve.

To make the chocolate pudding; lightly butter six 150ml (¼ pint) ramekins and line the bases with greaseproof paper. Melt the butter in a pan over a low heat. Add the dark chocolate pieces, remove from the heat and stir until the chocolate melts. In a bowl, whisk together the 3 eggs, the 3 egg yolks and the sugar, until the mixture becomes thick. Whisk in the chocolate mixture, then slowly whisk in the flour.

Half fill the ramekins with the chocolate mixture, place 3 raspberries on top and top up with the rest of the mixture, so that the raspberries are in the centre. Bake in a preheated oven at 180°C/350°F/Gas 4 for 15 minutes or until set. Meanwhile, make the compote of fruit; in a pan, mix together all the ingredients and gently warm over a low heat until the fruit beaks down.

To serve, remove the puddings from the ramekins and place in the centre of each plate, dust with icing sugar. Flood the plates with the sauce and place 3 spoonfuls of the compote around the pudding. Decorate with a sprig of mint.

*My favourite chocolate pudding recipe donated for your Cook Book was included in my most recent cookery book **'Big Kevin, Little Kevin'** because, as a self-confessed chocaholic, it is delicious to eat and great fun to cook!*

Annual visit of the Queens Dragoon Guards (Welsh Regiment) to the charity.

ROSS BURDEN

Ross Burden is Britain's hot chef who has gone from strength to strength since he burst on to the cooking scene as a finalist on Masterchef. He is stylish. Self-taught as a result of his mum's less than perfect cooking. 'The tastiest man in Britain'. Wine aficionado. A degree in Zoology! Writer. Traveller ~ giving him the tag of 'World Cook'. One of the UK's top 50 most eligible bachelors (Company Magazine) and voted No.1 in London by readers. Joan Collins hailed him as her 'favourite chef'. He is a regular 'A' list guest on the London scene and the polo circuit.

When he settled on London in the 80's, having run restaurants in New Zealand and London, and on the back of his TV success he started The Contemporary

Catering Company. His clients include film stars, heads of corporations and the Royal Family.

1999 was off to a flying start filming *Ross On The Range* in the US where he did everything from skiing, horse riding, skydiving, fishing, meeting Navajo Indians ~ and even some cooking. In New Zealand he is the subject of a documentary and recently filmed 40 *Ready Steady Cook's* there. He recorded a series in South Africa and in June he taught in a Tuscan Palazzo. In between all this he is developing two television programmes and researching his second book. This summer he has made a big departure from the cooking world to present National Geographic's series *Explorer's Journal* where he is able to utilise his other passion, natural history.

1998 saw *'Ross In Thailand'* for CFN and *'Ross' Foreign Assignment'* was repeated. His book *'At Home With Ross Burden'*, was published in October. The range of *Ready Steady Cook* merchandise was either launched or continued to sell in its thousands, with Ross as one of the faces used for promotion. He was a regular winner on *Ready Steady Cook* and *Celebrity Ready, Steady Cook. Through The Keyhole* visited his home in June and the show will be repeated in March '99. He appeared on BBC Wales' *Sing For Your Supper* and he is a frequent guest on game shows. In August he flew to New Zealand to get their version of *Ready Steady Cook* off and running and was hailed as the 'local boy done good.' For the remainder of '98 his commitments included filming a new prime time cooking series for transmission in 1999, a travel stand for *The Travel Channel*, guesting on several lifestyle/cooking shows, personal appearances from Lands' End to John O'Groats and hosting a cookery course in an Italian palazzo.

In 1997 he continued as a frequent winner on *Ready Steady Cook* as well as *The Big Breakfast*; Ch4's *Light Lunch* where he was the most requested chef; a stint as GMTV's foody; panellist on the BBC's quick *All Over The Shop* hosted by Paul Ross; the BBC *Good Food Show* and a host of press features. He helped to promote *Ideal Home Magazine's* state of the art kitchen at *The Ideal Home Exhibition*.

Among all this and the rounds of media interviews and personal appearances Ross still finds time to run his catering business, to pursue his interest in penguins, *yes penguins*, his passion for natural history and travel and to support *The Childrens' Wish Foundation*. Curiously, and unfortunately for a foody, Ross is allergic to nuts!

Spinach And Ricotta Gnocchi

Ingredients
25g butter
1 small onion, finely chopped
300g frozen spinach, thawed and thoroughly drained
Pinch salt
250g ricotta
90g flour
1 egg
80g grated Parmesan
¼tsp nutmeg

Method

Fry the onion in the butter and add the spinach and salt, continue to cook for five minutes. Beat the ricotta and flour and add the rest of the ingredients. Mix very well. Flour a large surface and form sausages of the mixture about 2cm thick. Cut into 2cm lengths, pinch in the middle (gnocchi means 'knee') and dust with flour. Poach in lots of salted water and serve with Parmesan or place in a buttered ovenproof dish, scatter with herbs and black pepper and Parmesan and bake for 20 minutes.

Christmas Puddings on sale in the Charity Gift Shop.

AINSLEY HARRIOTT

A insley Harriott ~ a Sarf London boy ~ has, over the last 40 years, been cooking up quite a career for himself in top restaurants, as a celebrities' caterer, on stage, radio and television as a singer and comedian and latterly as TV's most exciting personality chef.

Readers voted him Best TV Chef at the *TV Quick Television Awards* and in two recent polls, for *TV Times* and *Teletext*, he was voted favourite TV chef by a huge margin, Ainsley winning almost half the total vote. 'My aim is to make cooking fun,' says Ainsley, following the rules he learned from his late mother, Peppy ~ use fresh ingredients, have everything ready beforehand and never said 'It's too difficult'.

Aged 16, Ainsley got himself a job as a junior trainee at West End restaurant Verrey's, where he graduated to commis chef. He moved to the Strand Palace before taking a break to tour Europe as part of a musical duo (his show business talents being inherited from his musician/actor dad, Chester). Returning to England, he teamed up with partner Paul Boross to form *The Calypso Twins*, racking up several TV credits, a record release and a prominent position on London's New Comedy circuit.

But cooking remained Ainsley's first love and he continued to pursue a career in top hotels, gaining experience in all aspects of his craft. He also started his own catering company. 'It was an exciting period,' says Ainsley. 'One day I'd be creating posh nosh for Elton John; the next I'd be making steak and kidney pud with mash for Princess Margaret. I've been lucky to have worked at every level of the catering business ~ and I think that it's an enormous advantage to know how to make delicious beans on toast as well as Lobster Thermidor.'

It was during his spell as Head Chef of the Long Room at Lord's that BBC Radio asked him to present *More Nosh, Less Dosh* for R5. A call from *Pebble Mill* soon followed and Ainsley moved in to become resident chef on BBC TV's *Good Morning with Anne and Nick*. Next came *Ready Steady Cook*, which his popularity helped to make a ratings winner and he has since gone on to host his own highly-rated BBC TV series, *Can't Cook Won't Cook*. He has hosted *The National Lottery Live*, journeyed to Las Vegas for BBC1's *Holiday Memories*, appeared on *Food & Drink, You Bet!, Surprise, Surprise* and many other TV programmes.

In 1997, Ainsley's first solo series came to prime time BBC television. *Ainsley's Barbecue Bible* took him around the world, sampling and cooking the very best open air food. The companion book, published by the BBC, became the UK's number one best-selling hardback. 1998 saw his new series, *Ainsley's Meals in Minutes*, come to the BBC. Again, the series was accompanied by a colourful and stylish hardback book which also became an immediate chart-topper, selling more than 100,000 copies in its first two months in the shops. In the autumn of 1998 Ainsley hosted his first BBC1 prime time entertainment series *Party of a Lifetime*, throwing surprise parties for the unsuspecting public. 1999 sees the completion of two more major series for the BBC. *Ainsley's Big Cook Out* takes him on a culinary journey the length of the Americas. And BBC1 Saturday night entertainment's *The Hidden Camera Show* will take him to a brand new audience.

His first book ~ *In The Kitchen with Ainsley Harriott* ~ was published in Spring 1996 and his second ~ *Can't Cook Won't Cook*, published in March 1997 ~ went straight to the top of the BBC paperback charts. He also writes a weekly column for *TV Quick* and now presents *Ready Steady Cook* having taken over from Fern Britton. Ainsley spends any spare time with his wife, Clare, children Jimmy and Madeleine and dog, Oscar.

Char Char Chicken And Leek Pasta

Serves 4

Ingredients
350g/12oz spaghetti
1 pack of baby leeks, cooked and refreshed
6tblsp olive oil
2 boneless skinless chicken breasts, cut into 6 strips
1 lemon
75g/3oz Parmesan, grated, plus extra to serve
1 garlic clove, crushed
1tblsp tarragon, roughly chopped

Method
Heat the griddle pan. Cook the spaghetti according to the packet instructions.

Brush the leeks with 1 tblsp of oil, cook for 2-3 minutes on each side until slightly charred. Cover and set aside.

Place the chicken in a medium bowl, grate over the zest of the lemon and stir in 1 tblsp of olive oil, mix well, season with salt and pepper. Char-grill for 2-3 minutes on each side until golden brown.

Meanwhile make the dressing. Mix together the remaining oil, the juice of the lemon, Parmesan, garlic and tarragon, season with salt and pepper.

Drain the pasta and return to the pan. Pour over the dressing and gently fold through the chicken and leeks. Divide between four pasta bowls and garnish with shavings of Parmesan.

NICK NAIRN

Nick Nairn is Scotland's first celebrity chef and one of the country's most popular figures. His career started as a navigating officer in the Merchant Navy and he opened his first restaurant, Braeval, in 1986. Nick won a Michelin star in 1991 and was voted Scottish Chef of the Year in 1996.

His first TV series, *Wild Harvest*, was broadcast nationally in 1996, *Wild Harvest II* in 1997, and the third, one of Scotland's most popular programmes, *Island Harvest*, took Nick and his 43ft yacht 'Island Harvester', around the Outer Hebrides in February 1998.

He regularly appears on numerous radio and TV programmes including *Ready Steady Cook, Celebrity Ready Steady Cook, Who'll Do The Pudding?, Feeling Healthy*, and *Masterchef*.

In 1997 he opened Nairns, a 100-cover restaurant with 4 hotel rooms, in Glasgow, which was instantly acclaimed 'the hottest restaurant in Scotland' by the national press.

Nick also works as a chef consultant for several large international companies including *Pifco (Tower and Russell Hobbs), Compass* and *Seagram International (Chivas)*, and previously *Tesco*, and *Marks and Spencer*. *Nairns Cook School* opened in April 2000 and is already enjoying overwhelming public interest. *Nairns Anywhere* is the Outside catering section, catering for events such as the opening of the Scottish Parliament, and clients such as *J P Morgan, Compass, BT* and *Foodfest*, www.nairns.co.uk averages 1000 hits a week. *Nairns* is situated in an elegant Georgian townhouse at 13 Woodside Crescent and along with two dining areas, has four individually designed bedrooms. Recognised as a five star Restaurant with Rooms by the Scottish Tourist Board.

Cep, Smoky Bacon and Pea Risotto

Serves 6 hungry people

Ingredients
100ml (3fl oz) olive oil
1 medium onion, finely diced
2 cloves of garlic, crushed and diced
225g (8oz) carnaroli rice

150ml (5fl oz) white wine
25g (1oz) best quality dried Scottish ceps
4 rashers rindless streaky bacon, chopped into short strips
100g (4oz) peas, fresh or frozen
900ml (1¾ pints) chicken stock
25g (1oz) Parmesan cheese, freshly grated
25g (1oz) butter
2 tablespoons chopped flat leaf parsley, plus extra for garnish (optional)
Maldon salt
Freshly ground white pepper

Method

Soak the ceps in 500ml of warm water for about half an hour until they have visibly swelled and the water has turned a dark peaty brown.

Remove the mushrooms from the liquid (keep the mushroomy water) and drain well.

Using 1 tablespoon of the butter heated in a frying pan, sauté the mushrooms for a couple of minutes, then pour about 100ml of the mushroom liquid into the pan, turn up the heat and allow it to reduce with the mushrooms. Cook until all the liquid has been absorbed. Remove from the heat and keep to one side until you are ready to add them to the risotto.

In a separate large frying pan heat the olive oil. Add the bacon, onion and the garlic and cook over a medium heat for 6-8 minutes, until the bacon has lightly browned and the onion has softened. Then add all of the rice and stir well until it becomes well coated in olive oil and started to become translucent ~ this should take a couple of minutes.

Add the wine and 6 turns of the pepper mill and cook over a medium heat for about 4 minutes until the wine has been absorbed.

Pour in 750ml of the chicken stock and bring to the boil, stirring from time to time. Reduce the heat to a simmer and cook for 10-12 minutes, stirring occasionally.

Add the remaining stock and the mushrooms and bring back to a simmer for 8 minutes, until the stock has been absorbed, then add the butter, beat in the Parmesan and mix in thoroughly until it has all combined, then season to taste.

Garnish by topping with a sprig of flat leaf parsley and a few long curls of Parmesan.

LOTTE DUNCAN

L otte is the quintessential English Cook with a passion for the 'Darling Buds . . .' approach to England's culinary heritage.

She joined the *Ready Steady Cook* team in September 1998.

Since May, Lotte has become one of the regular chefs on *Gloria Hunniford's Open House* on Channel 5, with Gloria personally asking for her, and is also a regular guest on Sky Television's *The Living Room*, cooking anything from English summer ice-creams to Star Wars children's food!

Lotte welcomed back British Beef BBC1's *Vanessa Show*. She was asked to develop a recipe especially for the occasion. In April, Lotte was on BBC's *Webwise* programme, showing presenter Kate Humble a thing or two about Tudor food.

She presents regular slots on the *Food Network Daily* for the Carlton Food Network and will be presenting the Christmas Preparation items. She has also filmed *'Ideal Home Cooks'* With Nanette Newman for Pineapple Productions, again on Carlton Food Network. The series, entitled *English Food Revisited*, was aired from the first time in March 1998 and is often repeated.

Lotte broadcasts a monthly *Food and Drink* programme on BBC Thames Valley FM as the resident chef.

She is a regular at demonstrating at the *BBC Good Food Shows* in Birmingham and London for *Focus on Food*, supported by the Royal Society of Arts.

As well as television work, Lotte runs cookery demonstrations in some of Oxfordshire's and Buckinghamshire's finest period homes. She develops all her own original recipes. Lotte is also involved with her local *Farmers Market*. She is keen to promote local produce and British Farmers.

Cargo Homeshops sponsor Lotte and her demonstrations. She developed recipe cards for their shops which went nationwide in the summer of 1999. Lotte is also involved with Pru Leith and *The British Food Trust*. She has been asked to become part of a Task Group to develop a *British Culinary Archive* in Stafford, where the centre of culinary excellence will be built by the year 2003.

All this follows living and working in Switzerland, Los Angeles and Oxford, running a catering company and bringing up a beautiful daughter!

Lotte showed an early interest in cookery by becoming a finalist in the *Junior Cook of the Year'* competition in the early eighties. An 18-month old Cordon Bleu Cookery diploma course at Winkfield Place followed ~ where she gained distinctions.

She is 29 and lives in Buckinghamshire with daughter Daisy. Her father is the renowned cartoonist Robert Duncan who is responsible for her wonderful logo.

That's the story . . . so far.

A Very Excellent Syllabub Trifle

Serves 8

Ingredients

For the syllabub:
Grated zest and juice of 1 lemon
5fl oz (150ml) sweet white wine
1 tblsp of icing sugar
1 pint (570ml) double cream

For the trifle:
1 pint (570ml) milk
grated zest and juice of 1 orange
6 egg yolks
1tsp arrowroot
1lb (450g) Madeira cake
2tblsp sherry
8oz (225g) raspberries
4oz (110g) ratafias
2 tblsps brandy

To decorate:
3 yellow roses and 2 large sprigs of rosemary

Method
Two hours before making the trifle, soak the lemon rind, juice, icing sugar and white wine together from the syllabub ingredients.

Make a custard by heating the milk with the orange zest. Beat the egg yolks with the arrowroot and the sugar and when the milk is at scalding point, add to the egg yolks. Mix well and return to your saucepan. Heat very gently until thickened ~ _DO NOT BOIL. COOL._ Sprinkle with a little Castor sugar to prevent a skin forming.

Place half the cake at the bottom of your serving dish and pour over the sherry. Put the raspberries on top. Now the ratafias, the brandy and then the cooled custard. Now, put on the rest of the cake.

Make a syllabub by loosely whipping the cream and adding the lemon and wine mixture gradually to it. It should become the same consistency as custard. Pour over the top of the cake.

Now decorate with the flowers and rosemary.

Roscoff

Paul and Jeanne Rankin
Seven, Lesley House,
Shaftesbury Square, Belfast BT2 7QB

This dynamic husband and wife team run Roscoff, which was voted *Restaurant of the Year* in the BBC Good Food Magazine's 1996 Awards.

Since 1994 Paul and Jeanne have presented the 15-part network BBC1 TV series *Gourmet Ireland* ~ showcasing the best of Irish ingredients plus their own distinctive cookery talents. The third series was transmitted during 1996 and BBC Books have published two cookery books linked to the series. *Gourmet Ireland* was recently transmitted on the Public

Broadcasting Service in the USA and the accompanying book was published by KQED (USA). The series has also been sold to SBS in Australia, TVB in Hong Kong, TVNZ Pacific and TV2 in New Zealand, and to CBET Windsor in Canada.

Paul and Jeanne Rankin are eminently suited for this role. They have an easy style and an unpretentious attitude to food.

Roscoff's combination of ridiculously low-priced set meals, jazz music and laid back atmosphere has fuelled its popularity. In 1991 Paul and Jeanne were awarded Northern Ireland's first Michelin star and more recently Roscoff was named the *Courvoisier Restaurant of the Year*.

Paul has appeared on *Masterchef, Who'll Do The Pudding?* And *The Good Food Show*, and he is now a regular on BBC2's popular *Ready Steady Cook* as well as the evening version *Celebrity Ready Steady Cook.*

Jeanne is now a *Ready Steady Cook* regular and has guested a number of times on BBC2's *Food & Drink* as well as Channel 4's *Light Lunch.*

Paul and Jeanne published their third cook book complete with a jazz CD called *Hot Food, Cool Jazz* (Reed Books illustrated). Boxtree has just published Cooking with Ideal Home which is a compilation of their recipes from their monthly column in the same magazine.

Marinated Salmon Salad
With Lime And Pickled Ginger

Serves 4

Ingredients
450g very fresh salmon fillet
3 limes, juiced
1tsp salt
2tsp sugar
2 heads Little Gem lettuce, sliced
2tblsp pickled ginger (preferably Japanese) finely
sliced
2tblsp fresh coriander, chopped

For Sesame ginger vinaigrette:
2tblsp freshly grated ginger
100ml sesame oil (oriental)
100ml vegetable oil
50ml rice wine vinegar
2tblsp dark soya sauce
Salt and pepper

Method
To marinate the salmon: Trim the fresh salmon fillet
very well, cutting away any brown parts and make
sure that there are no bones.
Slice the fillet into approximately 16 thin slices and
lay these into a clean ceramic or stainless steel dish.
Whisk the salt, sugar and lime juice together in a
small bowl then pour it over the salmon pieces.
Allow this to marinate for 5-10 minutes depending

on how 'cooked' you prefer your salmon. The longer it marinates the less raw the salmon will look and it will turn lighter, a result of the marinade 'cooking' it.

To make the sesame ginger vinaigrette: Combine all of the ingredients together in a bowl, excepting the oils and whisk until the salt is dissolved. Slowly whisk in the two oils, and taste for seasoning. This vinaigrette will not emulsify completely.

To serve: Toss the Little Gem lettuce, fresh coriander and pickled ginger with a little of the vinaigrette. Divide between the serving plates, arranging neatly by pressing the salad into a 4in cooking ring. Drain the salmon slices and drape on top of the salad. Garnish with a little rosette of pickled ginger and a sprig of fresh coriander.

**Stan Stennett (Appeal Patron) selling chicks in Queen Street, Cardiff.
Charity 'Chick Knit' Easter 1997**

TRAVEL RECIPES

The St David's Hotel & Spa

Havannah Street, Cardiff Bay, Cardiff CF10 5SD
Tel: 029 2045 4045 Fax: 029 2031 3075
E-mail: reservations@fivestar-htl-wales.com

Situated on the waterfront of Cardiff Bay, the five-star St David's Hotel & Spa creates a striking landmark.

Visit Tides Bar & Restaurant for high quality cuisine using fresh, local produce prepared by Martin Green, former premier sous-chef at the London Connaught, whilst also enjoying the view across the bay.

Rump of Saltmarsh Lamb, Provençale Couscous And Rosemary-Scented Jus

Serves 4

Ingredients
120ml water
125g instant couscous
Salt and pepper
50ml Olive oil
3 x 70g courgettes
1 medium aubergine
1 red pepper
50g butter
12 cloves garlic
4 x 160g lamb rumps, boned and trimmed

For the garnish:
150ml lamb jus
Finely chopped rosemary
30g butter
Salt and pepper

Method
Boil water and add to couscous. Season with salt and pepper, mix with one tablespoon olive oil, stirring occasionally until cold. Put the rest of the oil in a pan, dice one courgette, half the aubergine and half the pepper in brunoise and sweat in oil.
Combine with the couscous, mould into four ramekins and reserve. Pass one courgette through a

mandolin, sweat in half the butter and season. Cut the remainder of the pepper, the last courgette and paysanne, sweat in butter until tender. Blanch garlic three times and fry in butter until golden. Season meat and roast for 8-10 minutes in oven. Drain fat from pan, reheat lamb jus, finish with rosemary and butter, season and pass through a chinois.

To assemble dish, reheat the couscous in microwave for 30 seconds. Place in centre of plate. Slice lamb and place on top of couscous. Place vegetables and garlic around plate. Coat lamb with the jus. Top with courgette spaghetti and rosemary. Serve.

Halloween Charity Fundraiser. The Alliance & Leicester Building Society, High Street, Cardiff

Cardiff Bay Hotel

**Cardiff Bay Hotel, Schooner Way, Atlantic Wharf,
Cardiff Bay, Cardiff CF1 5RT
Tel: 01222 465888 Fax: 01222 481491**

David Grindrod

One of Cardiff's leading hotels has appointed David Grindrod as head chef of its AA rosette restaurant.

David joins the Halyards restaurant at the Cardiff Bay Hotel having worked as head chef in hotels in the south of England and the Midlands.

David has lectured at Walsall College and presented his own culinary chat and phone-in show on local radio in the Midlands.

David's style is a fusion of classical and Mediterranean cuisine.

Saltmarsh Lamb With Chimoule

Ingredients
4 chumps of Saltmarsh lamb
2 lemons
2 limes
2oz coriander
Lemon zest
Lime zest
2oz parsley
4 garlic cloves
2oz ginger

For the sauce:
Cream
White wine
Coriander
2oz shallots

Serving suggestion
Roasted Mediterranean vegetables:
4 red peppers
4 yellow peppers
2 courgettes
2 red onions
2 aubergines

Seed peppers and cut lengthways, slice courgettes at an angle and slice the aubergine.

Crushed tarragon potatoes:
Virgin olive oil
Finely diced shallots
2lb boiled new potatoes
2oz tarragon

Method
Take the four lamb chumps and trim any excess fat
and sinew and if they are still very large then cut in
half lengthways, leaving a small piece of fat on one
side of the meat.

Mix together the juice and the zest of the lemons
and limes, add the parsley and coriander as well as
the 4 peeled garlic cloves and blend together with
2fl oz of olive oil.

Place the lamb on a metal tray or baking tray and
spread the marinade over the meat and gently rub
into the joints. Season with a little salt and black
pepper and then leave for between 12 and 24 hours,
depending on taste.

There are then two ways of cooking this dish:
For a dinner party, roll the chumps into separate
mini lamb joints and tie up with a piece of string,
place in an oven Gas 5/200° for approximately 30
minutes. About half way through the cooking add
the Mediterranean vegetables to the tray, cover
with foil and continue cooking.

Slice the potato and place in a saucepan with olive
oil, chopped tarragon and shallot, just lightly warm
through. In a separate saucepan sweat off the

shallots in a ¼ pint of white wine, bring to the boil and reduce by half. Then add ¼ pint of double cream and simmer until it starts to thicken. Finish with the chopped coriander.

To serve: Allow the lamb to rest for 5 minutes before slicing on a plate, of any juice comes off pour it through a sieve and add to the sauce, ensuring that no blood or fat goes through. Take the string off and you should be able to get 4/5 slices per piece. Using a 5cm ring press the potatoes into a ring in the centre of the plate and arrange the vegetables on top. Place the sliced lamb just to the side and drizzle the sauce over and around the lamb.

Note: *This is a real summer dish and can be done on a barbecue. Instead of rolling the meat place it flat on the barbecue. Do the vegetables in foil with olive oil and the potatoes as before.*

Blas ar Gymru

A Taste of Wales Restaurant
48 Cryws Road, Cardiff Tel: 029 2038 2132

Wales is a country of many contrasts. A land of majestic mountains and beautiful valleys. Yet bordered in the north, south and west by the sea.

We have our own language. It is a land of song. A land of musicians, writers and poets.

Food and drink form an important part of our nation's heritage. The need to retain information of the dishes which were synonymous with the way of life throughout Wales instigated the Blas ar Gymru bill of fare.

Here you can partake in the delights of the true Celtic dishes prepared and cooked to perfection.

Our produce is obtained locally each day, therefore allowing us to introduce other dishes when they are available in season.

Cig Oen A Mel
(Honeyed Welsh Lamb)

The sauce, which is made from the rich meat juices is delicately flavoured with cider and honey. The sauce is served unthickened.

Serves 6-8 people

Ingredients
1 x 3½-4lb leg of new season Welsh lamb, boned and rolled
Salt and pepper
1tsp ground ginger
Two good sprigs of fresh rosemary
6oz clear honey
½ pint dry cider

Method
Set the oven at Gas Mark 6/400°F/200°C. Line a roasting tin with foil, Rub the lamb over with the salt, pepper and ginger. Put the rosemary into the roasting tin and set the lamb on top. Coat the lamb with the honey and pour the cider around the joint. Roast in the heated oven for 30 minutes then reduce the heat to Gas Mark 3/325°F/170°C and cook for 1½-1¾ hours (depending on how you like your lamb served and, of course, the size of the leg)

basting occasionally. Remove the meat from the roasting tin and keep warm.

Pour the lamb juices from the roasting tin into a saucepan and skim off the excess fat. Simmer the juices until reduced and slightly syrupy, adding a little more cider if necessary. Taste the sauce for seasoning and serve with the lamb. Garnish with a small sprig of rosemary if available.

Just the ticket! Cardiff City Traffic Wardens support the Velindre and Cancer Research Wales development phase of the appeal

Hotel Gril Campanile

Caxton Place, Pentwyn, Cardiff CF2 7HA
Tel: 029 2054 9044

A French company with over 390 hotels throughout the UK and Europe.

Campanile is famous for its buffets of fresh fish, cold meats, various salads.

Book your birthday and receive a personally made cake *free of charge.*

Papillote Of Plaice

Serves 10

Ingredients
10 plaice fillets
¼lb shallots
Leeks
¼ltr white wine
Seasoning
¼ltr double cream

Method
Place a bed of raw leeks and shallots in foil.
Put the fillets of plaice on top.
Add the seasoning.
Mix the white wine and cream and pour into the foil.
Close the foil and cook in the oven at 200°C for 12 minutes.
Serve with grated carrot to add colour to the dish.

Vegetarian Chilli

Serves 10

Ingredients
300g green peppers
300g onions
3-4 cloves garlic
1 red chilli pepper
2tblsp vegetable oil
1.5kg tinned tomatoes

500g tinned kidney beans
500g tinned pinto beans
500g tinned sweetcorn
3-4tblsp chilli powder
1tblsp cumin
Salt

Method
Dice peppers and onions, chop garlic and red chilli.
Cook in oil until barely tender.
Add tomatoes and their juice.
Add drained kidney beans, pinto and sweetcorn.
Season with chilli powder, cumin and salt.
Bring to the boil, cover and cook until tender on medium heat.
Taste and season with salt and chilli powder.

(left) The Sarcona Kid - ex cancer patient who completed a sponsored cycle ride around the Gt Britain coast!

Le Gallois Y Cymro

**6-8 Romilly Crescent, Canton,
Caerdydd/Cardiff CF11 9NR
Tel: 029 20 341264 Fax: 029 20 237911
E-mail: le.gallois@virgin.net
www.restaurant-parc.co.uk/1/Le_Gallois.html**

Le Gallois ~ Y Cymro (translates to the Welshman) is a family run restaurant headed by Graham and Anne Jones. Their son, London trained chef Padrig Jones, heads the brigade in the kitchen.

Opened in June '98 the restaurant has already received several accolades and reviews worldwide. It has recently been awarded *AA Restaurant of the Year for Wales 1999-2000* in addition to the two AA Rosettes awarded after only three months of opening. It has also been awarded *Best Restaurant in Wales ~ 'Out to Lunch'* category by *The Red Book's 2000 Edition.* Le Gallois is currently in the round-up section of new restaurants recommended by *The Good Food Guide.*

Le Gallois presents Modern European food in a smart and friendly environment where you can be assured of personal attention at all times.

Prune And Armagnac Soufflé

Ingredients
50g unsalted butter
12 egg whites
300g Castor sugar
4dsp Prune and Armagnac soufflé base (see * below)
4 whole marinated prunes

Method
Grease four soufflé dishes well with butter and sugar. Place in freezer to set.

Preheat oven to 180°C.

Beat egg whites until they start to take shape then add ¼ of the sugar. When the sugar has mixed in add another ¼ and so on until all the sugar has been added.

Place the Prune and Armagnac soufflé base in a bowl and fold in egg whites.

Half fill the soufflé dishes with the mixture, place half a prune on top and then fill to the brim, scraping off evenly with a palette knife.

Cook in the oven for 8-10 minutes. The soufflé should be quite firm on the outside and lovely and moist inside.

Serve in the dish. Sprinkle with icing sugar and place half a prune on top.

*Prune and Armagnac soufflé base

Ingredients
500g marinated prunes
30g cornflour
100ml Armagnac
100g Castor sugar
50ml water

Method
Remove stones from prunes and blend in processor. Pass through fine sieve into a saucepan. Bring to the boil and then simmer.

Dissolve the cornflour in the Armagnac and add to the prunes. Stir and cook until it thickens. Continue cooking for a few more minutes. Remove from the heat.

Mix the sugar and water together and boil up to 121°C (hard boil). Add to the prune mixture and mix well.

Leave to cool. It is now ready to use.

New House
Country Hotel

Thornhill, Cardiff CF4 5UA
Tel: 029 2052 0280 Fax: 029 2052 0324

The peace and tranquillity of New House Country Hotel, spectacular setting and finest cuisine make for a perfect retreat to relax and unwind at the end of a busy day.

Roast Breast Of Guinea Fowl, Crushed New Potatoes And Caerphilly Cheese, Summer Vegetables In A White Wine Sauce

Serves 4

Ingredients
4 guinea fowl breasts
500g new potatoes
200g Caerphilly cheese, grated
175ml single cream
1 chicken stock cube
50g butter
Small bunch parsley
400g young carrots
125g broad beans, shelled
2 pkts baby sweetcorn
8 shallots
Glass dry white wine
1dsp plain flour

Method
Preheat oven to 200°C.

Peel and simmer potatoes in salted water until just cooked. Remove from the pan, drain and place in a bowl. Lightly crush the potatoes with a fork, add the grated cheese and a small knob of butter. Reserve.

Heat another knob of butter in a roasting pan on a fairly low heat, seal and season the guinea fowl breasts on both sides. Remove from the pan and set aside.

Sprinkle one level dessertspoonful of plain flour over remaining butter in the pan and stir in. Add a wine glass full of cream and an equal quantity of water in which the stock cube has been dissolved. Stir.

Place mousse rings in the roasting pan about 2cm apart. Fill mousse rings with potato and cheese mixture pressing in firmly with a fork.

Place a guinea fowl breast, skin side up, on top of each.

Spoon the vegetables around the mousse rings and simmer for two minutes.

Finally add a glass of white wine and place in the preheated oven at 200°C for 25 minutes.

Serve with a liberal sprinkling of chopped parsley.

Manor Parc
Country Hotel
& Restaurant

☆ ☆ ☆

☆ ☆ ☆

Thornhill, Cardiff
Tel: Cardiff (029) 20 693723 Fax: Cardiff (029) 20 614624

Set in mature grounds, this personally run hotel offers a warm welcome and professional service.
The Orangery Dining Room overlooks the grounds.
A relaxing room where you can enjoy excellent cuisine from a choice of speciality and seasonal dishes.

Poulet Sauté Stanley

Serves 6

Ingredients
1 chicken weighing about 3lb, cut in pieces
1tsp curry powder
½lb onions, sliced
A pinch of Cayenne
6oz mushrooms, sliced
4 slices of truffle
2oz butter
Juice of half a lemon
½ pint cream

Cooking Time: 1 hour

Method
Cook the chicken and onions together in the butter for about 15 minutes.

Add the curry powder and cook 3-4 minutes.

Mix well, now add the sliced mushrooms.

Cook for a further few minutes, add the cream, cayenne and lemon juice, cover and cook in a moderate oven, 375°F/Gas Mark 4 for 50 minutes or until chicken is tender.

Serve and garnish with the slices of truffle.

The Royal George
Hotel And Restaurant

Tintern, Chepstow, Gwent NP6 6SF
Tel: 01291 689205 Fax: 01291 689448

Nestled at the foothills of Tintern described by Wordsworth as *'The Most Romantic Valley in Wales'* you will find The Royal George Hotel, with award-winning gardens and The Angiddy River framing this near perfect location.

Steeped in history, this former coaching inn boasts a *Red Rosette* for its restaurant and was voted *Consort Welsh Hotel of the Year 1999.*

Famous visitors that have sampled The Royal George's hospitality are Neil and Glenys Kinnock, Ben Elton, Ken Dodd, Barry Humphries, Nina Myskow, Oliver Tobias and the cast of Casualty that included Robson Green.

Chicken Italian

Serves 4

Ingredients

4 x 200g (8oz) chicken supremes
50g (2oz) Mozzarella cheese, divided into 4
4 slices of Parma ham (or Prosciutto Crud ham)
1 bunch fresh basil
A little olive oil
2 cloves garlic, crushed
½ medium onion
5 tomatoes, de-seeded and de-skinned
1tsp sun-dried tomato paste
½ glass white wine
¼ pint double cream
1tsp white wine vinegar
Pinch of sugar
Salt and pepper

Method

Lay the supreme on chopping board, remove skin, but put to one side the fillet (which is the smaller, loose part of the meat).
Butterfly the supreme by making an incision down the centre from top to bottom, then run the knife down either side to form two flaps, one either side,

which should also resemble a pocket or envelope. Be careful not to cut right through the flesh.

Fold sides back and place a basil leaf inside, season and add the cheese, then place another basil leaf on top of the cheese, followed by the fillet, fold sides back over the fillet ~ encasing the cheese.

Wrap one slice of Parma ham around the supreme, brush with olive oil and wrap in foil. Place in a hot oven, Gas Mark 7/220°C for 30-35 minutes.

Whilst chicken is cooking make the tomato sauce by finely dicing the onion and tomato. Gently fry the onion and garlic in a little olive oil for two minutes without colouring. Add white wine and white wine vinegar and boil until the liquid has reduced by half. Then add the cream, tomato, sun-dried tomato paste and seasoning. Simmer until the sauce has thickened slightly. Just before service, check the seasoning and add remaining basil (roughly torn but saving 4 whole leaves).

Remove the chicken from the oven and unwrap the foil. Diagonally slice into 6 or 7 pieces but keep it as close together as possible. Pour one tablespoon of sauce onto the plate and fan chicken on top. Garnish with a deep-fried basil leaf or even just a fresh basil leaf.

Black Bear Inn

**Bettws Newydd, Near Usk,
Monmouthshire NP5 1JN
Tel: 01873 880701**

Food is the priority here, the remoteness of the place demanding an inventive approach, with just enough produce on offer to see out the night.

Spontaneous, individual cooking is definitely worth seeking out and Stephen Molyneux's reputation is such that if you arrive without a booking you might be disappointed and in any case you will need directions in order to find Bettws Newydd.

Monkfish With Stilton Apple

Ingredients
8oz monkfish fillets
1 apple
2oz Stilton cheese
½ pint cream
1 glass white wine
2oz butter
Crushed black pepper
Salt
Herbs

Method
Melt butter in wok or pan, add cut up pieces of monkfish, grated apple and fry for 2-3 minutes.

Then add white wine and cheese, finish with cream.

Reduce for 3-4 minutes then eat it with a nice glass of Chablis!

Serve with light, young new potatoes, salad, endive and yellow pepper dressing.

Allt Yr Ynys Country House Hotel And Restaurant

Walterstone, Near Abergavenny,
Herefordshire HE2 0DU
Tel: 01873 890307
E-mail: allthotel@compuserve.com
Website: www.allthotel.co.uk

Allt Yr Ynys (pronounced alt-ur-inis) is centred on a beautifully preserved mediaeval 16th Century manor house steeped in history going back to the time of Rhodri Mawr ~ King of Wales. The hotel is located in the foothills of the Black Mountains on the fringes of the Brecon Beacons National Park.

Lush lawned gardens lead down to the rivers Monnow and Honddu fronting the hotel.

The ideal setting for a wide range of outdoor and indoor pursuits centred on the hotel's own indoor heated swimming pool, sauna and spa bath.

We can cater for groups, corporate gatherings, seminars, leadership courses, etc.

Lavender And Mixed Blossom Honey Créme Brûlée

Serves 4

Ingredients
240ml double Jersey cream
160ml full fat milk
5 sprigs fresh lavender, washed and crushed
7 egg yolks
100g mixed blossom honey
4tsp brown sugar
Shortbread biscuits
Fresh washed sprigs of lavender for decoration

Equipment
4 x 3in ramekins
Mixing bowl and whisk
Saucepan
Baking tray

Method

Preheat oven to 170°C.

Mix the milk, double cream and lavender in a bowl and leave to infuse for one hour.

Gently bring the lavender/cream/milk mixture to the boil over a low heat. Meanwhile, whisk the honey and egg yolks together in a large bowl.

Strain the lavender/cream/milk mixture and slowly whisk into the egg yolks. Leave to stand, skimming off and discarding any foam.

Place ramekins in a baking tray half-filled with warm water. Fill the ramekins with the brûlée mix and bake in the oven for approximately 15 minutes or until set. Remove from the oven, leave to cool and then refrigerate.

To serve, sprinkle 1tsp brown sugar on to the top of each brûlée. Caramelise under the grill or gently with a blowtorch.

Serve immediately on doylied side plates with shortbread biscuits and sprigs of lavender as decoration.

The Orles Barn Hotel And Barn Owl Restaurant

off Wilton Roundabout, Ross-on-Wye HR9 6AE
Tel: 01989 562155 Fax: 01989 768470
E-mail: orles.barn@clara.net
Website: www.orles.barn.clara.net

The Orles Barn Hotel located just across the river from Ross-on-Wye is set deep in the Herefordshire countryside.

During the summer months there is cooking around the barbecue next to the large heated outdoor pool, in the very private 1½ acres of lush gardens.

Samantha and Rob guarantee good food, laughter, relaxation and something completely different.

Bobotie

(Pronounced Baboote)

Surely the best-known South African traditional dish, with a tasty combination of sweet and savoury ingredients.

Serves 8

Ingredients
1 slice white bread
250ml milk
1kg minced beef or mutton
1 medium onion, finely chopped
125ml (½ cup) seedless raisins
125ml (½ cup) blanched almonds
15ml (3tsp) apricot jam
15ml (3tsp) fruit chutney
25ml (2tblsp) lemon juice
5ml (1tsp) chopped mixed fresh herbs
10ml (2tsp) medium curry powder
5ml (1tsp) turmeric
10ml (2tsp) salt
10ml (2tsp) oil
3 eggs
4 bay or lemon leaves

Method

Soak bread in 125ml milk, squeeze dry and mix with minced beef.

Mix in all other ingredients except remaining milk, oil, eggs and bay leaves.

Heat oil in a frying pan and brown meat mixture lightly.

Turn out into a casserole.

Beat eggs with remaining milk and pour over meat.

Garnish with bay leaves and bake at 180°C until set.

Serve with plain or yellow rice.

Variation: Traditionally, bobotie was made with leftover meat from the Sunday roast. Mince the meat ~ mutton, beef or pork ~ and stir in other ingredients except bay leaves, eggs and milk. Proceed as above, reducing temperature to 150°C and baking for about 30 minutes.

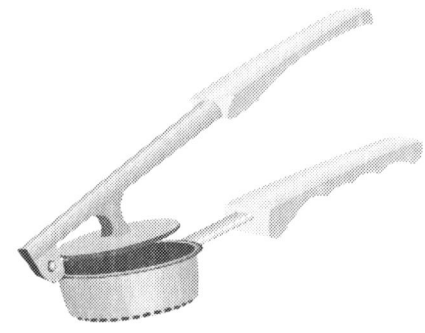

The Rosswyn Hotel

**The Market Place, High Street, Ross-on-Wye,
Herefordshire HR9 5BZ
Tel/Fax: 01989 562733**

The Rosswyn Hotel has the best of all worlds to offer the visitor, being literally a step away from the Market Place whilst retaining an old world atmosphere in its bar and restaurant areas.

The owner, personally supervises the interesting menu selection and whether you choose from the Dinner Menu or from the Bar Menu, your satisfaction will be guaranteed.

Unusual for such a centrally-placed hotel is its large private garden which is well used by locals and visitors alike during the summer months.

Tenderloin Of Pork With Orange, Redcurrant Jelly And Mango Chutney

Serves 4

Ingredients

700g (1½lb) pork tenderloin, well trimmed and cut into 1.25cm (½in) slices
15g (½oz) butter
15ml (tblsp) vegetable oil
Salt and pepper
2tblsp mango chutney
1tblsp redcurrant jelly
½ pint orange juice

Method

Place pork between 2 sheets of clingfilm and flatten with a rolling pin or mallet until thin.

Mix flour, salt and pepper then coat pork slices.

Melt butter and oil in a large frying pan or saucepan and brown pork slices on both sides.

Place browned pork into a casserole.

Add any remaining seasoned flour to frying pan and stir. Add orange juice gradually, stirring to thicken until smooth.

Add redcurrant jelly and mango chutney.

Pour over the pork and cook in a moderate oven for 10 minutes.

Mount Sorrel Hotel

Porthkerry Road, Barry,
Vale of Glamorgan CF62 7XY
Tel: 01446 740069
www.mountsorrel.co.uk
emailres@mountsorrrel.co.uk

Mount Sorrel has 43 bedrooms, a leisure club and four function suites catering for meetings, conferences, luncheons, dinner parties and wedding receptions.

Nigel, our Head Chef, creates his menus with locally bought produce from which a la Carte, table d'hôte, bar snacks and traditional Sunday lunches are available.

Sautéed Mushrooms With Stilton

Ingredients
Mushrooms
Butter
Stilton cheese, grated
Double cream
Chopped parsley

Method
Wash mushrooms and slice, sauté in pan with butter until soft.

Sprinkle with grated Stilton cheese, add double cream and chopped parsley, gently stir until cream thickens.

Serve in dish with garnish with lightly toasted French bread.

Delicious with a little garlic butter drizzled over toast.

Use as much or as little cheese as you like or alternatively use any cheese of your choice.

Lamb Burgers

Ingredients
1lb minced lamb
1 red onion, finely chopped
Generous helping of chopped fresh basil
2 cloves garlic, chopped
2oz sun-dried tomatoes
2oz toasted pine nuts
4oz grated Cheddar

1oz breadcrumbs
4oz spinach chopped
Salt
Pepper (milled)

Method
Mix all ingredients.
Mould to desired shape and size.
Grill or fry.
Delicious served with salad.

**Sid Golding ~ known to the charity as El Sid the
Master Badge Seller, advertising the mega hospital
Celebrity Auction in 1998.
Sid has raised many thousands of pounds for
charity over the past 20 years or so!**

Egerton Grey
Country House Hotel

Porthkerry, Nr Cardiff,
Vale of Glamorgan, Wales CF62 3BZ
Tel 01446 711666 Fax 01446 711690
Email info@egertongrey.co.uk
Web site www.egertongrey.co.uk

Set in a wooded valley away from main roads is the Egerton Grey Country House Hotel.

Carefully prepared fresh cuisine is served in the oak-panelled dining room which has pretty views down to the sea.

A wonderful setting in which to relax.

Baked Paupiette Of Plaice With Dill Breadcrumbs, Prawns, Gibbons And Cream

Ingredients

1 x 150g skinless fillet of plaice
1tblsp fresh white breadcrumbs
½tsp freshly chopped dill
100ml fish stock
50ml dry white wine
50ml single cream
25g cooked prawns
2 gibbons (spring onions) chopped on the slant
1 good pinch freshly chopped parsley
Salt and white pepper to taste
25g melted butter
25g flour (to coat fish)

Method

Place the fillet of fish, skin side up and roll up tightly from the tail then secure with a cocktail stick. Coat the fish in the flour removing any excess. Place onto a baking tray and brush liberally with melted butter.

Sprinkle the combined breadcrumbs and dill over the fish.

Bake in 200°C oven for approximately 8 minutes.

Meanwhile, in a saucepan, reduce stock by half, add the wine and reduce by half again.

Add the gibbons, prawns, parsley and reduce until the sauce coats the back of a spoon. Adjust the seasoning to taste.

Remove the fish from the oven, take out the cocktail stick, place onto a warmed plate and pour the sauce around the fish.

Members of the Welsh International Badminton Squad presenting the charity with their sponsorship money.

Huddarts Restaurant

**69 High Street, Cowbridge,
Vale of Glamorgan CF71 7AF
Tel: 01446 774645**

Huddarts is a small, family run, intimate and comfortable A La Carte restaurant, situated on the main high street in the ancient market town of Cowbridge.

They specialise in subtly combining the classical with modern techniques, to create dishes using fresh local produce in their own inimitable way.

Medallions Of Venison
With A Wild Mushroom Sauce

Ingredients

1½lb fresh lean haunch of venison (trimmed, sliced into 3-4 medallions per person, keep trimmings)
4oz fresh wild mushrooms (or 2oz if dried)

For sauce:
Venison trimmings
4 shallots, roughly chopped
2 glasses red wine
½ glass cherry brandy
1 pint beef stock
3tblsp ground nut oil
1tsp tomato purée
1tblsp cornflour mixed with a tiny drop of cold water to smooth paste
½ clove chopped garlic
2 bay leaves
2 sprigs fresh thyme
Salt and ground black pepper for seasoning

Method

Take thick-bottomed pan, warm with ½ ground nut oil, sauté venison trimmings till brown.

Add shallots and garlic, when soft add red wine, reduce by half.

Add beef stock, tomato purée, herbs and a little ground black pepper then allow liquor to simmer and reduce a little.

Gradually add cornflour, mix to simmering liquor till slightly thickened.

Keep warm.

Sauté fresh wild mushrooms off in separate pan with a hint of the oil until just soft.

Strain warm sauce onto mushrooms.

Add cherry brandy to taste. Adjust seasoning.

Seal seasoned medallions of venison in hot pan (not smoking hot) with remainder of oil until golden brown on both sides, best served pink.

To present, place a little pile of the wild mushrooms from the sauce in the middle of the plate and a little of the sauce around, arrange the medallions on top and enjoy!

Toasted Goats Cheese With Apricot Served with Redcurrant, Port And Orange Sauce

Ingredients
2 Pant Ysgawn Welsh goats cheese
4 slices thick cut wholemeal or granary bread
2 fresh firm apricots, diced (or dried pre-soaked)
1tsp finely chopped chives
4 salad garnish
1 x 2½in metal ring cutter (or scone cutter)

For the sauce:
4tblsp redcurrant jelly
Juice and zest of half fresh orange
Half measure of port wine

Method

In bowl mix goats cheese with apricot and chives, fork in lightly, do not over work as apricots will go mushy.

With ring cutter (or scone ring) cut out a circle of brown bread from each slice.

Toast till lightly browned on both sides.

Using ring cutter again, line with overlapping clingfilm, spoon in quarter of cheese mixture, lightly firm down, remove from cutter wrapped in clingfilm, chill in fridge. Repeat for other three portions.

For sauce: Warm the redcurrant jelly, port wine and orange juice and a little of the orange zest, simmer to reduce to syrup consistency, keep warm.

To assemble, place the ring on a flat baking tray, put toasted brown bread croute in the bottom of the ring, then remove clingfilm from a mould of cheese and place on top of bread croute.

Cheese is now ready for grilling. It would be ideal if there were four ring cutters as this would save time.

Prepare plates ready, with a little salad garnish.

Grill the goats cheese in the ring mould till nicely browned.

Meanwhile, place pool of warm sauce onto plates. Lift gently the whole ring and croute from underneath, place the toasted cheese on to the sauce, remove ring, serve and enjoy!

The Great House Hotel And Leicester Restaurant

Laleston, Bridgend CF32 0HP
Tel: 01656 657644 Fax: 01656 668892

The Great House (Ty Mawr) sometimes referred to as the Earl of Leicester's House, is a 15th Century Grade II, listed building.

The patio and walled garden have been laid out to give a perfect setting for weddings and private functions.

Our team of Top Chefs take a great deal of pride in their work. There is well-balanced menu which changes frequently and includes a vegetarian selection.

Roast Fillet Of Welsh Beef

Ingredients
4 x 8oz fillet or medallions of Welsh beef
8oz spinach
Roast potatoes
Roast shallots
Tomato relish
½ pint red wine sauce

For the relish:
¾ pint of vinegar
Pinch salt
pinch paprika
4 cloves garlic (chopped)
3 onions (chopped)
Olive oil
10oz Castor sugar
4lb of blanched tomatoes (de-seeded and chopped)

Place all the ingredients together in a pan and reduce for approximately 1½ hours until a relish consistency is obtained.

For the red wine sauce:
½ pint red wine
½ pint beef gravy

Method
Reduce the ingredients until only half of the original volume remains.

Spinach ~ Method
Sauté spinach with olive oil and season with salt, pepper and nutmeg.

Steak and Vegetables ~ Method
Seal off steak by frying lightly in a pan and season with salt and pepper.

Add the potatoes and shallots and roast together in the oven.

Continue cooking until the steak is to your liking, then remove it from the pan, but continue cooking the potatoes and shallots until they are cooked.

To serve place the spinach on a plate.

Place the steak on top of the bed of spinach then drizzle the relish around the plate.

Garnish the dish with the potatoes and shallots then finish the dish by dressing the steak with the red wine sauce.

Bryngarw House

**Bryngarw Country Park,
Brynmenyn, Bridgend, Mid Glamorgan CF32 8UU
Tel: 01656 729009 Fax: 01656 729007**

Close to the spectacular Glamorgan Heritage Coast and with walking trails leading from the park itself through beautiful valleys to dramatic hilltops beyond, Bryngarw enjoys a sense of seclusion.

The conservatory restaurant proudly serves the best of fresh produce.

By day offering light lunches and snacks. By night soft music and candlelight provide the setting for dinner.

Crispy Roast Salmon With Laverbread Omelette And Oatmeal Potato Cakes Accompanied By Cockle And Saffron Sauce

Serves 4

Ingredients
4 x 8oz salmon fillets (skin on) boned and descaled

For the coating:
Flour
Soft Butter
3fl oz cooking oil

For the omelette:
4 eggs
2oz Laverbread
Lemon juice
Chopped parsley
1tblsp double cream
1tblsp cooking oil
2oz cooked, chopped bacon

For the oatmeal potato cakes:
8oz mashed potato
2oz oatmeal
½oz chopped garlic
Chopped basil
1oz chopped onions
Flour for dusting

For the sauce:
2fl oz dry white wine
2fl oz vegetable stock or stock cube
4fl oz double cream
Seasoning
Lemon juice
Pinch saffron threads

Method
Potato Cakes: Mix the mashed potato with the oatmeal and cooked bacon. Sauté the chopped onions in a little butter until soft. Add to the potato mix.

Add chopped basil and mix thoroughly. Season to taste.

Roll into balls and flatten into rounds using a knife and then divide into four.

Dust lightly with flour and pan-fry on both sides until golden brown.

Place on a baking sheet lined with greaseproof paper and place to one side.

Salmon: Dip the skin side of the pieces of salmon in flour and shake off excess.

Using a pastry brush or knife, spread some of the softened butter onto the floured side of the salmon. Place on a plate and reserve in the fridge.

Meanwhile, heat a heavy-bottomed frying pan with the cooking oil in a medium heat until hot.

Place the chilled salmon into the frying pan, skin side down and shallow fry for about 3-4 minutes until golden brown and crispy. Carefully lift the salmon and flip over onto the flesh side and cook for 1-2 minutes. Season with a few drops of lemon juice.

Carefully remove the salmon and place on a baking sheet with the skin side up and place in a moderate oven for 3-4 minutes. The salmon should be pink in the middle.

At the same time, place the potato cakes into the oven.

Sauce: Place a saucepan on high heat and add the white wine.

Boil until nearly reduced, next add the vegetable stock and reduce by half.

Add the cream and bring to the boil and simmer until thickened to correct consistency (usually to coat the back of a tablespoon). Season to taste with salt and pepper and a couple of drops of lemon juice.

Add the saffron and leave to one side.

Omelette: Break open the eggs into a bowl. Season with salt and pepper and 2-3 drops of lemon juice. Add the cream.

Fold in the Laverbread and chopped parsley.

Heat 1tblsp of cooking oil in a large frying pan.

Place 4 egg poaching rings in the frying pan and divide the egg mixture between them.

Using a fork, mix the eggs as they cook. When slightly firm remove from the rings and, using a palette knife, swiftly turn them over and cook the other side.

Remove and place on a plate and put in the oven with salmon and potato cakes.

To serve: Reheat the sauce and bring to the boil.

Add cockles.

Arrange 4 clean plates.

Place the potato cakes in the centre of each plate and put the omelette on top of the potato cakes.

Lastly, place the salmon onto the omelettes with the skin side up.

Spoon the sauce around the arrangement and garnish with a sprig of basil and parsley.

The Grand Opening of the first CRW Charity Shop Whitchurch, South Wales.

Hurst Dene
Guest House

GUEST HOUSE

10 Sketty Road, Uplands, Swansea SA2 0LJ
Tel: 01792 280920

A warm reception awaits you at this recently refurbished, family run guest house, ideally situated for local attractions and transport routes.

Home cooked evening meals are an optional availability.

Pan Fried Cod With Parsley, Capers And Brown Butter

Ingredients
4 x 8oz cod fillets
Salt and ground black pepper
Flour
2tblsp olive oil
3oz butter
Handful capers
Handful chopped parsley
2 lemons

Method
Season cod and lightly dust with flour.

Add olive oil to pan. Place cod in pan and leave for 2 minutes.

When golden, turn over. When cooked remove from pan and keep warm.

Toss in butter, allow to melt and begin to colour slightly.

Add capers and parsley and swirl pan until butter begins to turn brown.

Squeeze juice of one lemon and remove from heat.

Swirl pieces in the pan and pour over cod.

Serve with lemon quarters, new potatoes and green salad.

Baked Fruit

Method

Place assortment of fruit (peaches, pears, nectarines, plums, figs, rhubarb) stoned and halved, sliced in shallow dish. Add splash of brandy or Cointreau and sprinkle with sugar. Roast in oven at highest temperature for roughly 4 minutes.

Serve with vanilla ice-cream or mascarpone cheese.

Charity support workers helping with the annual 'Tour de Cardiff' sponsored cycle ride.

Lakeside Hotel

P ★★★
HOTEL

Phoenix Way, Swansea SA7 9EG
Tel: 01792 310330 Fax: 01792 797535

Located just 1.5m from J44 of the M4 ~ a superb base from which to explore the numerous surrounding attractions.

Ample free car parking.

A la Carte and carvery food options from the restaurant, 24hr food in our licensed bar and lounge. Enjoy a workout, sauna or swim in our health club.

Pan-Fried Pork Fillet
With Gingered Apples

Ingredients

6oz pork fillet
2 rashers back bacon
1 seasonal apple
2tblsp sweet cider
1oz ginger
2tblsp olive oil
1oz unsalted butter
4 cherry tomatoes
2 basil leaves
½ pint demi glaze

Method

Trim excess fat off pork fillet then wrap with bacon.
Heat olive oil in a thick-bottomed pan and put in
pork fillet and season. Cook for 15 minutes.
Core apple and slice, then melt butter, add ginger
and apple and cook until soft and golden brown.
Once pork fillet has cooked remove from pan and
drain any excess fat from pan. De-glaze pan with
cider then add demi glaze. Adjust seasoning if
needed. Place sautéed apple on centre of plate then
slice pork fillet once diagonally and place on top of
the apple. Drizzle with cider sauce and garnish with
roasted cherry tomatoes and deep-fried basil leaves.

The White House Hotel

GWESTY
★ ★
HOTEL

4 Nyanza Terrace, Swansea SA1 4QQ
Tel: 01792 473856 Fax: 01792 455300
Website: www.thewhitehousehotel.co.uk
E-mail: reception@thewhitehousehotel.co.uk

Mike Jones trained at Hollings College, Manchester and has put in his BSc in Hotel and Catering Studies to good use during the past 12 yeas at the White House Hotel, Swansea.

The hotel has a reputation for excellent local food and exceptional service. Whether you're staying for an exciting week's holiday, or just for a short break, you'll not only get a warm welcome, but a fond farewell 'till next time!

Laverbread Bacon Bundles

This breakfast dish, which must be part-prepared in advance, has the advantage of easily cleanable utensils, as those of you who have pan-fried Laverbread will appreciate! It is also a novel and appealing way of presenting this delicious local dish.

Ingredients
¼lb fresh cockles
1lb fresh Penclawdd Laverbread (or tinned if fresh Laverbread is hard to come by)
10 rashers rindless best back bacon
Fine oatmeal to garnish

Method
Using a dessertspoon, place a few cockles into the base of approximately 10 plastic cups, add ½in layer of Laverbread then add another layer of cockles. Finish with a final layer of Laverbread. Top each cup with a teaspoon of oatmeal, place the cups on a tray and freeze overnight. When frozen, the Laverbread mixture can be removed from the plastic cups and stored in an airtight container in the deep freeze for up to 3 months.

When ready, remove the required number of frozen cakes, wrap each one with a slice of back bacon, starting with the tapered end of the slice. The bacon will freeze around the Laverbread, place into a ramekin and cook in the microwave for 3 minutes on defrost, then 4 minutes on cook for each bundle. Check the centre of the Laverbread which should be piping hot. Turn out onto the plate oatmeal side uppermost and serve with buttered toast triangles.

Some of the many Voluntary Charity Workers enjoying their annual Christmas Dinner.

Oxwich Bay Hotel

Gower Peninsular, Swansea, South Wales SA3 1LS
Tel: 01792 390329 Fax: 01792 391254

The former rectory of Oxwich until 1959, the hotel stands just yards from the beach in eight acres of private grounds, thirteen bedrooms, all en-suite, many with fantastic sea views.

A grand banqueting suite for weddings and lounge with terraced garden have all been transformed to make the Oxwich Bay Hotel one of the most popular venues on the Gower Peninsula.

With the appointment of top chef, Chris Keenan, food is top of the agenda, menus reflecting Chris' enthusiasm for freshly prepared food are served all day, every day, throughout the year (except Christmas Day)

Welsh Lamb With Cracked Pepper And Fresh Blueberries

Ingredients
4 x 6-7oz Welsh leg of lamb steaks
4oz chopped onions
1 cloves of crushed garlic
2fl oz raspberry wine vinegar
1 level tsp cracked black peppercorns
4fl oz fresh orange juice
4 heaped tsp redcurrant jelly
¾ pint water
Tomato purée
2tsp hoi-sin sauce
3tsp plum sauce
4oz fresh blueberries
Little oil for cooking
Little blanched orange zest
Salt and pepper

Method
Heat a little oil in an ovenproof dish, season the lamb steaks and seal them in the hot oil on both sides.

Add the onions and the garlic, keep them moving around the pan so that they soften and colour a little.

Sprinkle in the cracked peppercorns, then the raspberry vinegar, allow this to reduce almost completely before adding the fresh orange juice, the redcurrant jelly and the wine.

Stir in the tomato purée, hoi-sin and the plum sauce together with half of the fresh blueberries, have all this simmering nicely, then pour in the water.

Return to the simmer, season, cover and place in a hot oven for about 45 minutes.

Lift out the lamb steaks and keep warm, then reduce the liquid down to a light sauce texture.

Place each lamb steak onto a plate.

Just before you serve the sauce, check the seasoning, add the remaining fresh blueberries and just as they are ready to 'pop', pour the sauce over the lamb, finish with a little blanched orange zest and some crispy fried onions.

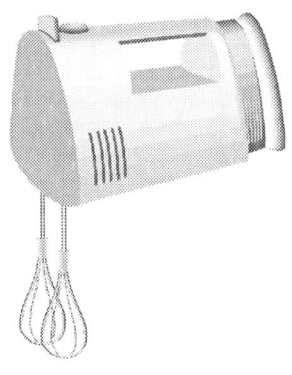

Bryncastell Farmhouse

Llanfair Road, Lampeter, Ceredigion SA48 8JY
Tel: 01570 422447

Join a traditional, bilingual Welsh farming family on their 140-acre riverside farm, in their luxury, purpose-built home, commanding panoramic views across the beautiful Teifi valley. Experience authentic Welsh recipes, using home-grown produce, expertly prepared and beautifully presented in generous quantities.

See the animals, walk the farmland or fish the riverbank, in an area of unspoilt natural beauty.

Carrot, Leek and Celery Soup

Ingredients
2oz (50g) butter
1lb (450g) leeks, finely chopped or sliced
½lb (225g) carrots, finely chopped
1 head of celery, finely sliced
2¾ pints chicken, lamb or beef stock
Salt
Sprig of thyme
Parsley
freshly ground black pepper
¼ pint (150ml) single cream

Method
Melt butter in large saucepan, add leeks, carrots and celery and fry slowly for 10 minutes to soften vegetables without colouring.

Add stock with salt and pepper; the amount will depend on seasoning in the stock. Bring to the boil, stirring. Cover saucepan, reduce heat, simmer for 30 minutes or until vegetables are tender.

Taste and check seasoning.

Just before serving add cream and stir gently.

Jalna Hotel

**Stammers Road, Saundersfoot,
Pembrokeshire SA69 9HH
Tel/Fax: 01834 812282
E-Mail: jalnahtl@aol.com
Website: www.jalnahotel.co.uk**

The Jalna Hotel is a comfortable 14-bedroomed 2-star hotel situated close to the Pembrokeshire Coast National Park path.

The hotel sits back about 200 yards from the picturesque harbour and beaches in the pretty village of Saundersfoot.

Bob and Jayne King, the resident proprietors take pride in offering traditional, well-presented British fayre.

Jalna Egg And Prawn Mayonnaise

Ingredients
1 hard boiled egg
Shredded lettuce
Sliced tomato and cucumber
Lemon twist
Prawns enough for 1 person
Mayonnaise Light for diets
Cayenne

Method
Place the shredded lettuce in the centre of the plate to create a little bed for the egg, the egg is halved to lie yolk down, surround with the prawns and decorate the dish with the sliced tomato and cucumber.

Cover the egg with the mayonnaise and sprinkle some cayenne pepper over the top, add a twist of lemon to finish.

Lovely as a starter or a light lunch served with a crusty roll or some brown bread and butter.

Skerryback

**Sandy Haven, Haverfordwest,
Pembrokeshire SA62 3DN
Tel: 011646 636598**

Skerryback is an 18th Century farmhouse, and a working farm, offering bed and breakfast.

Set in a sheltered garden, adjoining the Pembrokeshire coast path, it is an ideal situation for walkers and bird lovers exploring the secluded coves and sandy beaches of the area, and is only a short drive to Martins Haven to catch the boat to Skomer Island to see the puffins.

The two attractive double bedrooms, one being en-suite, look out across horses grazing in the meadow.

Breakfasts are a treat, the perfect way to start a day of strenuous walking or just relaxing on the nearest beach.

Garlic Mushroom Croustades

Ingredients
4 slices white bread
¾ pint basic white sauce
1tblsp oil
1 medium onion
1 or 2 garlic cloves
1lb mushrooms
A little grated cheese
Seasoning to taste

Method
Cut crusts off bread and make into rounds to fit 4in paté tins.

Butter both sides of bread and fit into tins and bake until crisp.

Fry onion and garlic in oil until just tender, add mushrooms.

When cooked combine with white sauce and fill croustades, sprinkle with a little grated cheese and put under the grill until just brown.

Delicious as a starter or vegetarian dish.

Dolau Isaf Farm

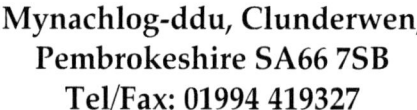

**Mynachlog-ddu, Clunderwen,
Pembrokeshire SA66 7SB
Tel/Fax: 01994 419327**

Peaceful farm with superb views, nestling in the
Preseli Hills.
Meals home-made with own or local produce.

Melon With Ginger
Chicken Breasts
With Mushrooms And Cream

Ball or chop a melon, add a little ginger syrup and chopped stem ginger on the top.

Chicken Breasts

Gently sauté 2 chopped cloves of garlic in butter with a little oil to prevent burning.

When lightly coloured, fry 2 chicken breasts until cooked. Turn half way through.

Put chicken breasts aside to keep warm and fry sliced mushrooms ~ use a little more butter if necessary.

Pour double cream over the mushroom mixture. Cook on high for a short time until mixture thickens and pour over chicken breasts.

Serve immediately with fresh vegetables and new potatoes.

Note: *This recipe can be halved or increased to cater for any number.*

Lochmeyler Farm Guest House

**Pen-y-Cwm, Near Solva, Haverfordwest,
Pembrokeshire SA62 6LL
Tel: 01348 837724 Fax: 01348 837622**

Lochmeyler Farm Guest House is located in a 220-acre working dairy farm 3 miles inland from the coastal footpath.

Meals are prepared by Mrs Morfydd Jones from fresh farm produce including vegetarian.

Welsh cakes are provided daily in the rooms.

Sticky Toffee Pudding

Ingredients

For the pudding:
3oz (75g) butter
5oz (150g) Castor sugar
2 eggs
6oz (175g) self-raising flour
6oz (175g) chopped dates
6fl oz (175ml) boiling water
½tsp vanilla essence
2tsp coffee essence
¾tsp bicarbonate of soda

For the sauce:
6oz (175g) soft brown sugar
4oz (110g) butter
6tblsp double cream

Method

For the pudding: Place chopped dates in a bowl with the boiling water and place in a microwave for 2 minutes until they boil.

Remove from the microwave and add the vanilla essence, coffee essence and bicarbonate of soda and put to one side.

Cream the butter and sugar until pale in colour.

Gradually add the beaten eggs a little at a time.

Fold in the flour and then add the date mixture.

Turn into a baking tray lined with bakewell and bake for 25 minutes until golden brown.

Method

For the sauce: Place all the ingredients in a saucepan and heat gently until the sugar has dissolved.
Do not boil.
To serve, cut the pudding into portions, pour the sauce over and serve with whipped cream.

Members of the Blackwood & Dist Scout Movement presenting their sponsorship cheque to the charity.

Whitehouse

**Pen-y-Cwm, Nr Solva, Haverfordwest,
Pembrokeshire SA62 6LA
Tel/Fax: 01437 720959**

S et in a quiet rural location 1½ miles from the coast.
Awarded *'Best off the Beaten Track'* by the Red Book
~ Eat well in Wales.

Lamb, Leek And Laverbread Casserole

Serves 6

Ingredients

1 kilo Welsh lamb, cubed (I prefer leg meat)
1 small onion, sliced
4-6 leeks, sliced
200gm Laverbread, fresh or tinned
3 bay leaves
1 bouquet garni
200ml white wine
400ml lamb stock
200ml single cream
Salt and pepper

Method

Toss the lamb in seasoned flour then brown lightly in a small amount of olive oil.

Set aside in an ovenproof casserole.

Soften the onion and then return the lamb to the pan together with the leeks, bay leaves, bouquet garni, wine and stock.

Bring to the boil, transfer to casserole and put into the oven on 180°C (Gas Mark 4) for 1 hour.

Remove and stir in the Laverbread, return to the oven for ½ hour.

Add the cream before serving.

Llangloffan Lamb Crumble

Serves 4

Ingredients

350g (12oz) minced Welsh lamb
30ml (2tblsp) Olive oil
1 medium onion, chopped
15g (½oz) flour
15ml (1tblsp) tomato purée
300ml (½ pint) lamb or beef stock
Salt and pepper to taste

For the topping:
50g (2oz) butter
100g (4oz) flour
50g (2oz) grated Llangloffan cheese
2.5ml (½tsp) dried mixed herbs

Method

Heat the oil in a pan and then brown the lamb. Mix in the flour, tomato purée then add the stock and seasoning. Turn into shallow ovenproof dish and set aside.

Run together the flour and butter until like breadcrumbs, stir in the cheese and mixed herbs. Spread the crumble over the meat.

Bake in the oven at 190°C (375°F) Gas Mark 5 for 45 to 60 minutes.

Quite rich in flavour so serve with plain steamed vegetables.

Lower Haythog

GUEST HOUSE

Spittal, Haverfordwest, Pembrokeshire SA62 5QL
Tel:/Fax: 01437 731279

For a taste of real country life, join us at our 13th century farmhouse on a working farm, with a friendly atmosphere.

The farmhouse exudes charm and character and offers tasteful and comfortable accommodation.

As *'Farmhouse Food'* award winners, we offer a wide variety of cuisine using the best of local produce.

Baked Avocados with Cockles

Serves 4

Ingredients
4 spring onions, finely chopped
2tblsp breadcrumbs
1tblsp parsley, chopped
2tblsp natural yoghurt
3tblsp mayonnaise
4oz cockles
2 avocados
1tblsp lemon juice
Salt and pepper
1tsp Dijon mustard
1 egg white
2oz grated cheese

Method
Mix the spring onions, breadcrumbs, parsley, yoghurt, mayonnaise and cockles together.
Cut the avocado in half and stone. Scoop out most of the flesh, leaving ½in in shell. Rub the inside of the shell with half the lemon juice. Mash the avocado and remaining lemon juice together and add to the cockle mix. Season to taste with salt, pepper and mustard. Whisk egg white until quite stiff and fold in grated cheese. Pile on top of avocado, cook in an oven 150°-175°C for approximately 20 minutes or until well-risen and brown. Serve garnished with lemon twists.

Ramsey House

**Lower Moor, St David's, Haverfordwest,
Pembrokeshire SA62 6RP
Tel: 01437 720321 Fax: 01437 720025**

Ramsey House is a 4-star guest house situated in a quiet convenient location on the outskirts of Britain's smallest city, St David's.

Catering exclusively for non-smoking adults, proprietors Mac and Sandra Thompson have earned themselves a reputation for fine food and wines with a distinctly Welsh emphasis.

Smoked Trout Paté

Makes 16 x 2oz portions

Ingredients
1lb boneless smoked trout fillets
12oz butter, very soft but not melted
4oz low fat yoghurt
4tblsp lemon juice (approximately 1 lemon)
½tsp black pepper
Little salt but taste first

Method
Mix all ingredients together thoroughly. This will leave recognisable pieces of smoked trout. A food processor may be used but this will give a much smoother texture ~ the choice is yours!

I use an ice-cream scoop for neat portions to serve with a salad garnish and lemon twists. Brown toast or oatcakes should accompany the paté.

Note: Smoked trout paté freezes well. Open freeze the portions then store up to 2 months in airtight bag or box.

The Old Court House
Vegetarian Guest House And Walking Holidays

Trefin, Pembrokeshire
Tel: 01348 837095

The Old Court House is a 200-year-old Pembrokeshire cottage, located in the peaceful village of Trefin.

The sunny south-facing garden looks out across rural farmland.

Meals are prepared using local produce to provide delicious vegetarian and vegan food.

Creamy Leek Croustade

A wonderful dish of contrasting flavours and textures

Serves 4-6

Ingredients
For the base:
6oz fresh wholemeal breadcrumbs
3tblsp vegetable oil
4oz grated cheese
4oz mixed nuts, ground
½tsp mixed herbs
1 clove garlic, crushed
1tsp wholegrain mustard
Salt and pepper

For the topping:
2 medium red onions, peeled and sliced
3 medium leeks, peeled and sliced
1 clove of garlic (or to taste)
2tblsp olive oil
½pkt sun-dried tomatoes
4tblsp white wine
3tblsp Marscapone
Salt and pepper
Fresh basil leaves

Method
Preheat oven to Gas Mark 4/180°C.

To prepare the base:

Mix the nuts, grated cheese, breadcrumbs and dried herbs together in a bowl.

Mix the crushed garlic, mustard and oil together and combine thoroughly with the dry mixture.

Press the mixture down well into a lightly greased, deep tray, approximately 8in x 12in. Bake for 15 minutes until golden and crispy on top.

To prepare the topping:

Heat the oil and sweat onion, leek and garlic together for 10 minutes on a low heat.

Add the wine and sun-dried tomatoes, cover and continue to simmer until tender.

Stir in the Marscapone.

Pile topping onto cooked base and serve immediately, garnished with fresh basil leaves.

Chocolate And Ginger Flapjack
A quick and easy recipe for all the family to enjoy!

Makes 16 slices

Ingredients
8oz margarine
6oz golden syrup
6oz demerara sugar
1lb rolled oats
2tsp ground ginger
Chocolate to decorate

Method

Preheat oven to Gas Mark 4/180°C.

Place margarine, syrup and sugar into a saucepan and melt over low heat (or melt in a bowl in the microwave).

Stir in the oats and the ginger and mix well.

Transfer into a greased tin, approximately 8in x 11in and press down well.

Bake in the centre of the oven for 30-40 minutes until golden brown.

Take out and leave to cool before cutting into slices.

Melt the chocolate in a bowl over a pan of boiling water or in the microwave. Decorate the slices with drizzles of melted chocolate.

Remove from the tin when cold.

Store in an airtight tin.

Note: *Will freeze if required.*

The first annual Velindre And Cancer Research
Wales Charity 'Chick Knit'.
Norman Wisdom getting acquainted with one of
the chicks!

Chapel Farm

**Castlemartin, Pembroke, Pembrokeshire
SA71 5HW
Tel/Fax: 01646 661312
E-mail: chapelfarm@aol.com**

Situated in the National park overlooking the sea, Chapel Farm is a family dairy farm of about 260 acres.

The large, comfortable farmhouse combined with excellent home-cooking creates relaxing holidays.

Apple And Marrow Chutney

Makes about 8lbs

Ingredients
4lbs prepared marrow
2-3oz salt
3lb apples
1lb onions
1½oz pickling spice
2½lb brown sugar
1½lb-2lb sultanas

Method
Peel marrow and remove seeds.
Cut into small pieces.
Put in bowl, sprinkle with salt.
Leave for 12 hours.
Drain liquid. Put in large saucepan or preserving pan.
Peel and chop apples and onions.
Add all ingredients placing spices in a muslin bag.
Bring to the boil.
Stir well.
Reduce heat to simmer.
Cook until thick.
Remove spices.
Spoon into warmed jars and seal.

Fresh Fruit Pavlova

Ingredients
6 egg whites
Pinch salt
12oz Castor sugar
2tsp cornflour
1tsp vanilla essence
2tsp vinegar

For the filling:
1 pint whipping cream
1 orange, peeled and segmented
1 red apple, cored and sliced
1 kiwi fruit, peeled and sliced
1 banana, peeled and sliced
6 green grapes, halved
Lemon juice

Method
Draw two circles 8-9in in diameter on greased silicone non-stick paper. Place on two baking sheets. Beat egg whites and salt until stiff. Beat in half the sugar. Mix cornflour with rest of sugar and fold into mixture, with vanilla and vinegar. Divide between circles and smooth over. Bake at 250°F/120°C Gas Mark ½ for 40-50 minutes or until firm on outside.

When cool, peep off paper. Spread one circle with cream, whipped. Top with other circle. Spread over more cream. Sprinkle fruit with lemon juice, arrange over cream. Decorate with remaining cream.

**Barclays Bank Staff visiting the charity office
with their sponsorship cheque following
a local fund-raising day**

Hammonds Park Hotel

Narberth Road, Tenby SA70 8HT
Tel: 01834 842696 Fax: 01834 844295
E-mail: bryndraper@compuserve.com
Internet: www.hammondshotel.co.uk

Hammonds Park is a family hotel owned by the Draper family.

Bryn, from Pontypridd, met Shirley in her hometown, Wellington, New Zealand and their two daughters Anne and Gwen were born there.

The family came to live in Wales in 1981 and bought Hammonds Park in 1991.

Hammonds Park is 2-star AA, 5-15 minutes walk from the town and beach.

If you have fond memories of New Zealand, or have wanted to visit, Hammonds Park gives you the chance to see, taste and sample New Zealand's culture.

New Zealand Maori Kisses

Ingredients
4oz butter
4oz sugar
2 eggs
8oz flour
2tsp baking powder
1 cup chopped dates
2dsp cocoa
1 cup chopped walnuts

Method
Cream butter and sugar, add eggs, beat well.

Stir in dry ingredients, mix in dates and nuts.

Using a teaspoon, scoop generous portions onto a cold greased tray.

Bake in a moderate oven 350°F/180°C/Gas Mark 4 for 10-15 minutes. When cold join together with the following:

Sift 8oz icing sugar, cream 4oz butter, add ½ the sugar gradually until creamy and fluffy, beat in 1 tablespoon sherry alternating with the remainder of the sugar. Stir in 4-5 drops vanilla essence.

New Zealand Lamingtons

Make or buy square of Madeira cake.

Cut into squares.

Make up a jelly, red or yellow.

Dip cake squares into the still warm jelly and then dip in coconut.

Leave to set and dry.

Split top and fill with a little jam and whipped cream.

**Local hospital charity fete workers
taking a well earned breather!**

Ivy Bank
Guest House

Harding Street, Tenby, Pembrokeshire SA70 7LL
Tel: 01834 842311

The Ivy Bank Hotel is a fine Victorian 4-star guest house in the historic town of Tenby.
Five minutes walk to the sea front.
Holders of professional hotel and catering qualifications.

St Clements Cheesecake

Ingredients

8oz Digestive biscuits
2 lemon jellies
Evaporated Milk (Carnation)
1oz Castor sugar
4oz butter
1 lemon (juice and rind)
10oz cream cheese
2 tins mandarins

Method

Crush biscuits and mix in melted butter. Press into the base of a large loose-bottom cake tin. Put in fridge to cool.

Melt 1 jelly in microwave on low setting until melted but not hot.

Add the rind and juice of 1 lemon.

Mix the evaporated milk on a medium setting mixer until thick and creamy.

Turn mixer down low, add Castor sugar, cream cheese then melted lemon jelly/juice, mix until smooth.

Stir in by hand 1 tin of drained mandarins.

Spoon onto biscuit base and leave in fridge overnight.

Next day decorate top with mandarins.

Melt 1 lemon jelly in microwave (without water).

When runny add ½ pint cold water. Gently pour on top.

(I do this while it is in the fridge so that the mandarins don't float off).
It will be ready to eat a couple of hours later.

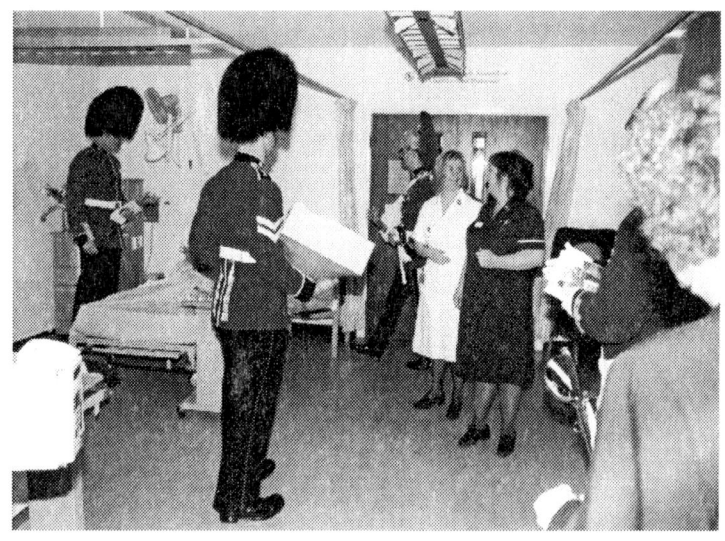

Queen's Dragoon Guards annual St David's Day visit to the hospital.

Plas Hyfryd
Country Hotel

**Moorfield Road, Narberth,
Pembrokeshire SA67 7AB
Tel: 01834 869006 Fax: 01834 869008
E-mail: david.jones30@virgin.net**

Plas Hyfryd, a delightful mansion is situated in Narberth, the heart of Pembrokeshire.

Our menus are prepared for you by the Plas Hyfryd's outstanding chef, who is renowned for his innovative cuisine.

Our comfortable lounge bar is an ideal atmosphere to relax in before or after dinner.

Guinea Fowl 'Plas Hyfryd'

Ingredients
1 breast 7oz (170g) guinea fowl
1 shallot, finely chopped
3-4 button mushrooms, sliced
2 rashers smoked streaky bacon, thinly sliced, grilled until crisp
1 measure of Calvados Apple Brandy
3fl oz dry white wine
½ small eating apple, peeled, cored, thinly sliced
3fl oz (75ml) double cream
Salt and pepper to taste
Few drops lemon juice
Vegetable oil for cooking

Method
Heat a heavy-bottomed pan with a little oil in and sauté the seasoned guinea fowl for 3-4 minutes on each side. Remove from the pan and place in an ovenproof dish in a moderate oven. Add the shallots and mushrooms to the pan, cook for 1-2 minutes, add the Calvados and white wine and reduce the liquid by half.

Add the sliced apple and finish the sauce with the cream and a little lemon juice to taste.

Take out the guinea fowl, slice and arrange on a plate, pour the sauce over and sprinkle on the crispy bacon.

Serve!

Cnapan

**East Street, Newport, Pembrokeshire,
Dyfed SA42 0SY
Tel: 01239 820575**

Cnapan is one of the finest listed houses in Newport. Around the house you will find bookcases full of maps, local information, books, magazines and a variety of games to ensure endless hours of interesting reading and fun.

Our sunny and sheltered garden is always in use, especially by those enjoying tea or a drink outside.

Mother and daughter work together in the kitchen forever looking for new ideas for mouth-watering dishes to present in the restaurant!

The evening meal we consider to be something of an occasion with much thought and care going into our menu and into the choosing of fresh local fish, meat and vegetables.

Celtic Pie

Ingredients
For the oat base:
4oz (125g) margarine
2tblsp water
4oz (125g) oats
3oz (75g) wholemeal flour
Salt

For the filling:
7½oz (210g) fresh or tin of Laverbread
2 fresh tomatoes
Tarragon or other herbs
1 onion, sliced in rings
Olive oil for frying
4-6oz (125-175g) tasty farmhouse cheese, sliced
5oz (150ml) natural yoghurt
1 orange, juice and zest
2 eggs
4tblsp tinned sweetcorn
Salt and black pepper

Method

Make the base. Melt the margarine, add water then the oats, flour and salt. Stir briskly.

Line 8½in (21cm) flan dish using fingers to press the oat mixture out.

Make the filling. Arrange a layer of tomatoes on the base of flan and sprinkle over a favourite herb.

Fry onion rings in a little olive oil and place on top of tomatoes.

Cover with slices of cheese.

In a bowl mix Laverbread, orange juice and rind, yoghurt, eggs and sweetcorn.

Pour this mixture over the cheese. Season.

Bake at 400°F/200°C/Gas Mark 6 for 40-45 minutes until mixture is set. Garnish with chunks of orange.

Tregynon Country Farmhouse Hotel

**Gwaun Valley, Nr Fishguard,
Pembrokeshire SA65 9TU
Tel: 01239 820531 Fax: 01239 820808**

In the heart of the Pembrokeshire coast national park, we have an attractive 16th Century farmhouse surrounded by peace and beauty of unspoilt countryside with its abundance of wildlife and flowers. This is 'Bluestone Country', the land from which came the famous Bluestones of Stonehenge and parts of Tregynon are built with this stone.

Tregynon is renowned for the variety of its menus, specialising in traditional delicacies, wholefood and vegetarian.

Lord Cawdor's 'Rack' Rack Of Lamb With Rosehip, Rosemary And Elderberry Sauce

4 racks of lamb (Preseli lamb, of course!), French trimmed ~ ask your butcher to do this! (Each rack being 3-4 joined chops in size)

Bake the racks in a roasting tin or Pyrex dish for 25 minutes at Gas Mark 5/375°C.
Remove from the oven and press stuffing onto the fat of each rack.
Return to the oven and cook for a further 25-35 minutes depending on whether you prefer your lamb slightly pink or well done.
Attach 'chef's hat' on one of the bones.
Serve with Rosehip, Rosemary and Elderberry Sauce.

For the stuffing:
3tblsp butter or margarine
2tblsp lemon juice
Breadcrumbs made from 4 slices wholemeal or granary bread
½tsp each thyme and marjoram
Salt and ground pepper

Method
Mix all the ingredients together with seasoning to taste.

For the sauce:
1oz butter or margarine
1 heaped tblsp plain flour
2tblsp rosehip essence
1tblsp elderberry wine
¼ pint apple juice
1tsp rosemary

Method
Melt the butter/margarine and add the flower to make a roux. Blend in the rosehip essence, elderberry wine, apple juice and rosemary. Allow to stand for at least half an hour for the flavour of rosemary to penetrate, then bring to the boil stirring all the time until thickened.

If too thick add more apple juice. Pour through a sieve to remove the rosemary.

Peter's note: Despite the fact that unless you are a qualified surgeon and know where to make your first incision, you may feel disadvantaged. I am convinced the only way to cook and serve a rack to retain all the flavours is whole.

Boozy Medieval
Bread And Butter Pudding

Ingredients

4 thin slices of muesli bread (any bread can be used but the result is not the same)

Butter

Home-made orange marmalade

2oz sultanas

½ pint milk

¼ pint single cream

2 eggs

2 tablespoons rum*

1 orange, finely grated rind

1tblsp light muscavado sugar

Nutmeg, ground or grated

Method

Spread the bread with the butter and marmalade and cut into triangles.

Arrange, buttered side up, in a greased ovenproof dish until the bottom of the dish is covered. Sprinkle with sultanas then add alternate layers of bread and sultanas until the dish is full.

You can top the pudding with sultanas but be careful they don't burn during cooking.

Heat the milk without boiling. Beat the eggs with the rum and orange rind and gradually add the milk and cream, whisking well. Pour over the bread and leave to stand until the bread has absorbed the milk.

Further eggs and milk can be added in the same proportions depending upon how moist a pudding you prefer.

Sprinkle sugar and nutmeg on the top and bake at Gas Mark 4/350°C for about half an hour, until golden and the mixture is set.

Peter's Note: I always emphasise this pud as being 'laced with rum' or, as one guest put it, 'heavily!' In my opinion 2 tablespoons should only be a very rough guide ~ according to taste!

The recipe is taken from their own cookery book 'Dining with Angels'.

Seaview Hotel

Seafront, Fishguard, Pembrokeshire SA65 9PL
Tel/Fax: 01348 874282

Family run hotel and restaurant on seafront. Convenient for ferry, coastal path and countryside. Hot and cold food served all day. Panoramic views.

Gwaun Valley Pasties

Ingredients
3 medium courgettes
1lb leeks
4 pieces celery
Fresh ground black pepper and salt
1 clove garlic
Fresh double cream

Method
Finely chop leek, celery and garlic.

Grate courgettes.

Fry gently in olive oil until soft, season, add cream and simmer for two minutes.

Place in savoury pastry rounds and crimp pasty style.

Brush with egg and bake in a moderate oven until golden.

Alternatively, serve without pastry as a tasty vegetable with a main course.

By omitting the cream it will make a good vegetarian or vegan main course dish.

Sir Benfro
Country Inn/Hotel

**Sandy Haven Road, Herbrandston, Milford Haven,
Pembrokeshire SA73 3TD
Tel: 01646 694242 Fax: 01646 697020**

Old style Pembrokeshire farmhouse.
Large garden, close to beaches, golf course.
En-suite rooms. Excellent cuisine.

Monsen Special Vegetarian Bake

Serves 4

Ingredients
2 firm tomatoes
3 courgettes
Selection of mushrooms (oyster, shitake, button)
1 aubergine
2 peppers, red and orange
1 medium onion
Fresh spinach (should be washed 12 times changing water every time)
½ pint double cream
1 fresh chilli, optional
Salt and pepper to season

Method
Take an 8-12in ovenproof dish.
Slice courgettes and aubergine and place around the outside and along the bottom of the dish, 1 layer, then slice the mushrooms, tomatoes and peppers, place these on the next layer.
Shred the fresh spinach, place in the middle.
Slice tomatoes, place on top of spinach.
Any of the above ingredients which may be left over can be sliced and placed on top.
If chilli is required, chop and sprinkle it with seasoning.
Pour on cream and bake in oven Gas Mark 5, middle shelf for approximately 20-25 minutes.

If desired grated cheese can also be sprinkled on top to give a nice cheesy, crusty topping.

Bananas Flambéd In Brandy

Best buy are slightly under-ripe, medium size bananas chosen for their firmness.

Ingredients
4 under-ripe bananas
4dsp brandy
2oz demerara sugar
1 pint double cream
4 brandy snaps (may have to buy in packs of 6)
2oz butter (not margarine)

Method
Place butter in a thick-bottomed frying pan (large enough to take 4 bananas).
Lightly melt the butter, peel bananas and slice lengthways and place in pan.
Sprinkle with demerara sugar and lightly fry for approximately 2-2½ minutes.
Remove bananas onto warm plates.
Increase heat so butter and sugar boil, add brandy at arms length and ignite the flame or if electric use taper.
Once flames have doused themselves (ie alcohol has burned off) add cream and cook for a further 2 minutes or until cream has thickened.
Pour over bananas and dress with brandy snaps.

Warpool Court Hotel

RECOMMENDATIONS

AA ★★★ ◎◎
RAC ★★★ (Food Merit)

Best Loved Hotels of the World
Johansens
Ashley Courtenay
Signpost
Family Welcome Guide
and other leading hotel guides

Wales Tourist Board
👑👑👑👑
Highly Commended

St David's, Pembrokeshire
Tel: 01437 720300 Fax: 01437 720676
Email warpool@enterprise.net

The hotel commands a southerly outlook over one of the most beautiful coastal stretches in Europe. Glorious sea views from the restaurant provides an ideal atmosphere for enjoying the extensive range of mouth-watering cuisine.

Grilled Seabass On Jasmin Rice And Vanilla Butter Sauce

For the fish:
1 x 2lb seabass, filleted, skin on and scaled.
Season with salt and lemon juice.
Grill for about 4 minutes under a hot salamander.

For the rice:
5oz Jasmin rice
2 chopped shallots
½oz butter, unsalted
1 bayleaf

Sweat down the shallot in the butter with the bayleaf. Add the rice and warm in the butter.
Cover with water and cook with a lid on for 10 minutes.
Season as required.

For the sauce:
Prepare a fish stock with the seabass bones, thyme and the seeds from a vanilla pod.
Reduce to a syrup and whisk in 2oz of unsalted butter. Finish with chopped parsley and a squeeze of lemon juice.
Arrange the seabass on the rice and pour the sauce around.
Serve with lightly cooked selection of vegetables.

The Old Vicarage Country Guest House

Moylegrove, Near Cardigan, Pembrokeshire
SA43 3BN
Tel: 01239 881231 Fax: 01239 881341
E-mail: davidhphillips@compuserve.com

Relax and revitalise in our elegant Edwardian home with large lawned gardens, set in an elevated position above the sensational Ceibwr Bay.

Perfect centre to discover the delights of Bluestone Country.

Salmon Steaks
With Mustard Cream Sauce

A simple to prepare dish featuring a delicious sauce not normally associated with salmon.

Ingredients (per serving)
For the salmon:
Salmon steak 6-7oz
Tblsp dry white wine
Sprig fresh tarragon
¼ bayleaf
Salt and black pepper

For the sauce:
¼oz butter
1fl oz double cream
Tsp wholegrain mustard

Method
Take a large sheet of foil and lay it in a shallow baking tin. Wipe salmon steaks and place side by side on foil.

Pour over wine and lay tarragon and bayleaf on salmon. Sprinkle with salt and pepper.

Fold over the foil and seal to make a parcel and place in a preheated oven 350°F/Gas Mark 4 for 25 minutes. Remove and keep warm.

Meanwhile prepare the sauce. Melt the butter in a pan, add the cream and mustard and bring to the boil. Simmer until the sauce thickens ~ about 10 minutes.

To serve, carefully remove the herbs and skin from the salmon steak and discard. Place steak on a plate and spoon over the sauce.

A SELECTION OF FAVOURITE RECIPES IN AID OF
VELINDRE HOSPITAL CANCER RESEARCH WALES.
Compiled by Marks & Spencer, Cardiff.

**Front cover of the first charity cook book
published and sold by Marks & Spencer,
Queen Street, Cardiff.
The cartoon donated by 'Gren' of the
South Wales Echo newspaper.**

Penbontbren Farm Hotel

**Glynarthen, Near Cardigan/Aberteifi,
Dyfed SA44 6PE
Tel: 01239 810248 Fax: 01239 811129**

Located in the quiet parish of Glynarthen, Penbontbren has been 'discovered' by many people seeking good food and comfort.

Use of local products create dishes based on traditional Welsh recipes.

Penbontbren Farm Hotel, formed from Victorian outbuildings on the family farm, has received a *Welsh*

Tourism Award and *Schroeders Bank* runners-up prize for Welsh medium-sized business of the year.

Smoked Fish Terrine

A 'local' starter.

Ingredients
2 fillets smoked mackerel, skin removed
2 fillets smoked trout
4oz smoked salmon

For the dressing ~ mix together:
1tsp wholegrain mustard
Salt and pepper
1tsp sugar
2tblsp vinegar
1tblsp olive oil

Method
Flake the fish, ensuring that all skin and bones are removed. Mix.

Mix all the ingredients for the sauce together and fold into fish mixture.

Serve with lettuce leaves, lemon wedges and accompanied with toast.

The Griffin Inn

**Llyswen, Brecon, Powys, Wales LD3 0UR
Tel: 01874 754241 Fax: 01874 754592
E-mail: info@griffin-inn.freeserve.co.uk
Website: www.griffin-inn.co.uk**

Savour the rich tradition of rural hospitality from four generations of The Stockton family, with country cooking from produce of the land, rivers and seas.

Glanwye Sauce For Salmon
Or Hot Smoked Salmon

Ingredients

4 salmon steaks or hot smoked salmon (about 150g each)
1tblsp cornflour
1tblsp mustard
1dsp sugar
Salt and pepper
1 egg, whisked
25g butter, softened
450ml milk
250ml vinegar
2 spring onions, chopped
½ cucumber

Method

Put the fish on a lightly oiled tray and grill for just 2-3 minutes or pan fry skin side down for the same time. Lightly season.

Warm the milk and vinegar, mix all dry ingredients and pour in the warm mix, blend then return to the saucepan.

Bring back to the boil to thicken and cook gently for a few minutes, mix the egg and butter, beating well. Take the pan off the boil and add the sugar.

Chop the spring onion quite finely with the cucumber (chopped skin on to retain crunch).

Leave to cool and serve with hot smoked salmon or salmon.

Griffin Marinaded Game

Ingredients
1 kilo venison cut into 4 steaks

For the marinade:
100ml oil
500ml red wine vinegar
100ml wine vinegar
200g chopped celery/carrots/onion
50g chopped parsley stalks
6 bay leaves
Sprigs rosemary and thyme
Zest of one orange
6 crushed juniper berries

Method
Bring the marinade ingredients to the boil in a pan and leave to simmer for 10 minutes. Cool completely before using. Place steaks into marinade and leave in a cool place or fridge for 48 hours.

Pan fry over a high heat to seal, then turn down to a medium heat for 7-8 minutes. Leave to rest for a further 10 minutes in a warm place before serving.

This is to ensure a pleasant peakness is obtained throughout and that all the meat juices are collected in the pan, rather than running all over the plate.

Serve with a caramelised shallot and onion ragout and a glaze sauce using the meat juices and marinade.

Caramelised Shallots

400g whole shallots
Oil
100ml marinade juice
50g Castor sugar
A little water

Onion Ragout

Ingredients

400g onions, sliced into rings, 5mm thick
Oil
100ml medium sherry
100ml marinade juice

Method

Fry the onions until slightly brown. Add the sherry, cover and cook, stirring occasionally for 10 minutes. Add the marinade and cook for a further 30 minutes until a jam-like consistency is reached.

Chef's Tip: If you have a whole haunch of venison, hang it in a cool place, ideally a cellar for 4-8 days so the meat becomes dark red. Trim skin and sinew and cut into steaks, then marinade.

Guidfa House

AWARD WINNER

**Crossgates, Near Llandrindod Wells,
Powys LD1 6RF
Tel: 01597 851241 Fax: 01597 851875
E-mail: guidfa@globalnet.co.uk
Website: www.guidfa-house.co.uk**

This stylish Georgian Guest House has earned an enviable reputation for its comfort, good food and service.

Set in the very heart of Wales, 3 miles north of Llandrindod Wells.

Guidfa Lamb

Ingredients

1 x best end of neck of Welsh lamb, boned
100g Welsh lamb's liver, chopped
25g butter
1 small onion, peeled and finely chopped
25g sultanas
50g fresh white breadcrumbs
1tblsp fresh mixed herbs (or 1 level tsp dried herbs)
Salt and pepper

For the coating:
50g plain flour, seasoned with salt and pepper
1 large egg
75g dried breadcrumbs
25g lard or dripping

Method

Fry onion in butter over a low heat until soft, add the liver and fry until sealed, then stir in the fresh breadcrumbs, sultanas and herbs with plenty of seasoning and leave to cool.

Lay out the meat, spoon the cold stuffing in the centre of the joint and roll it up so that the fat is on the outside. Secure it in place with cocktail sticks.

Put the flour, egg beaten with a little salt, and the breadcrumbs on to separate plates, then coat the joint first in the flour, then the egg and finally in the breadcrumbs to that the meat is completely covered.

Put the joint onto a plate and leave it in a cool place for one hour.

Heat the dripping in a roasting tin and fry the joint quickly so it browns on all sides, then transfer it to a moderately hot oven, Gas Mark 5 or 375°F/190°C for 1¼-1½ hours or until the meat is cooked.

Baste the joint every 30 minutes to create a crispy surface.

Remove the cocktail sticks and serve cut into slices.

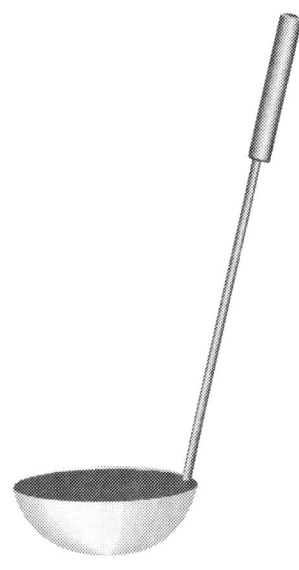

Drovers Arms

Howey, Llandrindod Wells, Powys
Tel: 01597 822508 Fax: 01597 822711
E-mail: info@drovers.co.uk
Website: wwwdrovers.co.uk

The Drovers is a 'superb' inn (as quoted in the *Rough Guide to Wales*) located in the heart of mid-Wales.

David and Janet Day have been successfully running the Drovers Arms since 1987.

Food is fresh and home-made using the best of local produce. They have been recognised as a good food inn by the *CAMRA Good Pub Food Guide* for a number of years.

The dining area is no smoking, and they care passionately about their food and look forward to giving their customers a real Taste of Wales.

Boned Shoulder Of Lamb, Pot Roasted And Served With Mint And Madeira Sauce

Serves 4

Ingredients
1 boned shoulder of Welsh lamb
1 onion, cut in half
1 carrot, roughly chopped
1 stick of celery, cut in half
1 bouquet garni
200ml dry white wine
Seasoning
250ml sweet Madeira
1tblsp chopped mint
1tblsp tomato purée

Method
Remove excess internal fat and tie up. Place in roasting tray, add wine, vegetables, bouquet garni and seasoning. Cover with foil and roast at Gas Mark 3 (150°C) for 2 hours.

Remove shoulder and keep warm, strain cooking juices into saucepan and reduce by 50%. Add Madeira, mint and tomato purée and simmer for a further 5 minutes.

Slice meat thickly (¼in), place on a circle of mashed leek and potato, pour sauce round and serve with braised red cabbage.

**Estee Lauder charity evening 1999
- Mariot Hotel, Cardiff**

The Bell Inn

Glangrwyney, Near Crickhowell, Powys NP8 1EH
Tel: 01873 810247 Fax: 01873 812155

The Bell Inn is a family-run 17th Century former coaching inn situated on the main A40 road between the two market towns of Abergavenny and Crickhowell.

We have a delightful 50-seater oak-beamed restaurant which serves a range of home-cooked bar meals plus a more elaborate a la carte menu. In addition, we have 5 en-suite bedrooms including a 4-poster room for those special occasions.

We also offer private fishing on the River Usk together with a large beer garden for the summer months.

Locally, there are many activities on offer such as walking, horse riding, golf, hang-gliding to name but a few.

Supreme Of Brill
With Mussels And Spinach

Serves 4

Ingredients
1kg mussels, cleaned
250ml dry white wine
1kg spinach
A little unsalted butter
4 fillets of Brill, about 800g
200ml double cream
Pinch of saffron
Salt and pepper

Method
Put the mussels in a large saucepan with the wine over a high heat. As soon as the shells open, tip the mussels into a colander over a bowl to catch the cooking liquid.

Strain the liquid through a fine sieve into a clean pan and place over a high heat to boil until reduced by half. Leave to cool. Shell the mussels and place in a bowl with a little of the cooking liquid. Keep chilled.

Wash the spinach, boil for 1 minute then refresh in cold water, drain and squeeze dry.

Preheat the oven to 180°C/350°F/Gas Mark 4.

Butter a gratin dish and arrange the spinach in the dish to form a bed for the brill. Dot the fish with more butter, cover loosely with foil and bake for 12-15 minutes or until the fish is opaque.

While the brill is cooking, add the cream to the reduced mussel liquid. Bring back to the boil and simmer until slightly thickened. Add the saffron and season to taste.

When the brill is nearly cooked, add the mussels to the sauce and heat through gently. Pour over the fish and serve from the gratin dish.

**Cwmbran Police HQ Officers getting in
on the fund-raising act.**

Red Lion Inn

**Llanfihangel-nant-Melan, New Radnor,
Powys LD8 2TN
Tel: 01544 350220**

Nestling in the Cwm Neigl, some three miles west of new Radnor, on the A44 is the village of Llanfihangel-nant-Melan. The old whitewashed drovers inn there has been dispensing sustenance and refreshment to weary travellers for centuries.

The combination of traditional Welsh and modern cookery, using local fresh produce has brought the Red Lion many awards, including being named as one of the *'Restaurants of the Year'* in the *Good Food Guide* 1997 and again for 2000.

In addition to good food and ale, there are three separate en-suite rooms, a perfect base to explore the beautiful surrounds of Radnorshire and the Welsh Marches.

Red Lion's Peppered Duck

Ingredients
1 duck breast
1 heaped tsp cracked black peppercorns
A little brandy
1tblsp duck gravy (or chicken)
1tblsp double cream
Salt

Method
Trim the duck breast of excess fat and sinews.
Salt on both sides and cover with peppercorns, pressing them well into the duck.
Heat in a pan on a medium heat.
Place the duck skin side down into the pan.
As the fat starts to run, turn up the heat and seal the duck on both sides.
Return to skin side and cook in hot oven (Gas 7-8) for 5-10 minutes depending on preference.
Remove from oven and allow to rest skin up in a warm place.
Tip off the excess fat from the pan, flame with brandy, add the gravy and reboil.
Add the cream, reduce slightly and season to taste.

Pour sauce onto plate, carve duck thickly and arrange around sauce. *Blasus Iawn.*

The 'Royal Oak' Nelson, supporting the cancer appeal.

Pentre Bach

**Llyngwril, Near Dolgellau, Mid Wales
Tel: 01341 250294 Fax: 01341 250885
E-mail: velindre@pentrebach.com
Website: www.pentrebach.com**

You can relax at Pentre Bach known for its organic vegetables grown in a walled kitchen garden, its organic fruit grown in the 'woodland garden' following the principles of permaculture, plus free-range/GMO-free eggs.

The use of home-grown produce in an imaginative way plus other local food and goods wherever possible has brought awards like *'Best bed and breakfast in Britain'* from BBC Radio 4's *The Food Programme* in 1996 and *'Mid Wales Cook of the Year'* in 1994.

Pentre Bach, with magnificent sea views and the mountains behind it, offer 3 en-suite bedrooms, candlelit dinners and breakfast at literally any time!

Apple Sunset

Serves 4

Ingredients
1 large cooking apple, peeled, cored, sliced
Cinnamon
4tblsp apple jelly, diluted with a little apple juice or water, mixed well
Or apple juice cooked with a little arrowroot to thicken it, coloured slightly with red or orange food colouring, cooled
28 stoned dates
4tblsp natural wholemilk yoghurt
Handful toasted, flaked almonds
1 washed organic, red-skinned, crisp eating apple. (Cox or Braeburn)

Method
Cook the apple gently with a tablespoon of water until it is a thick purée. Flavour with cinnamon and cool.
Prepare the jelly or juice.
Cut up the dates with scissors, each into about 5 pieces.
Assemble everything at the last minute.
Mix the yoghurt into the dates (do not overmix or the yoghurt will go brown) and make a mound of it

in the middle of 4 flat dessert plates. Cover with the apple purée.

Core and thinly slice each quarter of the unskinned eating apple into 7 slices. Tuck these under the dates, as the rays of the sun. Spoon the jelly between the apple slices on half of the plate. Sprinkle the flaked almonds on the top of the apple purée and serve.

Note: *If you use unsweetened apple juice, there is no added sugar in this recipe. For vegans, substitute vanilla soya dessert for the yoghurt. For low fat diet, substitute low fat yoghurt.*

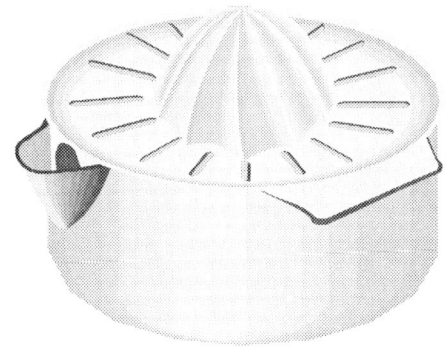

The West Arms Hotel

**Llanarmon, Dyffrn, Ceiriog, Llangollen,
North Wales
Tel: 01691 600665 Fax: 01691 600622
E-mail: gowestarms@aol.com**

Centuries ago, cattle drivers coming down from the Welsh hills by way of three tracks (now passable roads) that converge on The West Arms were wont to shelter, rest and refresh their cattle at the inn en route to Chirk, Oswestry and Wrexham markets.

Inglenook fireplaces with roaring fires, low ceilings and uneven floors, cuisine that is prepared by Grant Williams and his brigade whose passion in life is to produce wonderful food with loving care, creativity and with all local produce (wherever possible), make for an unforgettable visit to the Ceiriog Valley, an oasis of restfulness, beauty and tranquillity.

Ceiriog Valley Pheasant

A breast of local pheasant stuffed with a Stilton mousse wrapped in bacon and sliced with a pear and shallot confit laced with a locally-made damson wine sauce.

Ingredients
8oz Stilton
500g double cream
3 pears, poached in wine and diced
1 egg white
1tblsp chopped chives

Stilton Mousse ~ Method
Place Stilton (without the rind) into a food processor and blend until smooth. Add the double cream until a dropping consistency is reached. Remove from the blender and place into a bowl. Add half the finally diced poached pear and chopped chives, some black pepper and fold in half the beaten egg white, making sure the consistency is still fairly firm. You may leave this in the fridge overnight. (But do not add the egg white until you are ready to use the mousse.)

Confit Of Pear And Shallots

Ingredients
4 shallots, finely chopped
6fl oz cider vinegar
4oz demerara sugar
1tblsp shredded mint
Small handful of redcurrants
Remaining poached pears

Method
Sweat finely chopped shallots until soft and transparent in a thick-bottomed pan, add cider vinegar and demerara sugar and reduce until almost all liquid has evaporated. Stir in remaining diced poached pears, redcurrants and shredded mint. Remove from heat and set aside to cool. (Can be made the day before.)

The Pheasant

Ingredients
2 breasts of pheasant, skin removed
Selection of herbs, chopped
Juice of 1 orange and lemon
8fl oz olive oil
6 pieces of rindless streaky bacon
½ medium white onion, 1 sprig celery, ½ medium carrot, all diced
1 bottle home-made damson wine or any fruity wine
1 pint game stock or convenience chicken bouillon

Method

Marinade the breasts of pheasant for 24 hours in olive oil and a good selection of chopped herbs, lemon and orange juice.

Remove the breasts from the marinade and make an incision along one side of the breast but not all the way.

Fill this with Stilton mousse and wrap the peasant up with rindless streaky bacon.

Seal in a very hot heavy-bottomed frying pan, with a touch of oil and place in an oven (200°C) for 10-12 minutes or until it feels firm to the touch.

Remove from the pan. Use this pan with the juices in to soften the diced onions, carrots and celery on the top of your stove. Add the damson wine, but stand well back as this will flame. (This action burns the alcohol but concentrates the flavour of the wine.)

When the flame has died own, add creme fraiche and mix it in.

Reduce this to a nice consistency, strain and correct the seasoning and set aside.

To assemble the dish, slice the pheasant once on an angle, set upon the pear and shallot and confit and drizzle with the sauce, garnish with chives and redcurrants. *Bon Appetite.*

Hotel Maes-y-Neuadd

Talsarnau, Near Harlech, North Wales LL47 6YA
Tel: 01766 780200 Fax: 01766 780211

Wales' top team of chefs, the *'Welsh National Culinary Team'* was formed in 1993. Since its formation the Team has grown from strength to strength and through its ambition to strive for success is now recognised worldwide.

The Welsh National Culinary Team consists of 12 members who are either Welsh, work in Wales or have links with Wales. But importantly, all have the same goals to win and in doing so, help the food and drink industry from Wales.

The Team consists of: *Peter Jackson*, Team Manager, Hotel Maes-y-Neuadd, Near Harlech, *Trefor Jones*, Team Captain, Celtic Manor Hotel, Near Newport, *Graham Tinsley*, Vice Captain, St David's Park Hotel, Ewloe, *Colin Gray*, Pastry Chef, Barons Patisserie, Cardiff, *Sarah Duggan*, Faculty of Business, Leisure and Food, University of Wales Institute Cardiff.

Through the Welsh National Culinary Team's fund-raising efforts, not only have the Team been able to promote Welsh food abroad but have been able to support some of the UK's major charitable organisations and good causes.

Parcels Of Spinach And Oysters

Serves 4

Ingredients
8 large leaves spinach
8 oysters
Juice and zest of 1 lime
20ml vermouth
Salt and pepper
200g unsalted butter
20g chopped chervil

Method
Wash the spinach and trim the stems. Blanch in salted water for 30 seconds, refresh in iced, cold water.
Spread out onto clingfilm, form into four parcels.
Divide the oysters between the spinach and make four parcels and wrap in the clingfilm.

Steam for 4 minutes and while this is going on make the sauce.

In a pan reduce the lime juice with the vermouth by half.

Turn the heat down and whisk in the butter, check the seasoning and add the chervil just before service.

Unwrap the parcels and pour the sauce round it and serve.

Peter Jackson, Team Manager,
Welsh National Culinary Team

Martins
Award-Winning
Restaurant
With Rooms

11 Mostyn Avenue, Craig-y-Don, Llandudno,
North Wales LL30 1YS
Tel: 01492 870070 Fax: 01492 876661

SPECIAL OFFER
Martins would like to offer purchasers of the cook
book 10% discount off accommodation on production
of the book

A warm welcome and delicious 'award-winning' cuisine await you at this Victorian Town House 'Restaurant with Rooms' (former home of the Arch Druid of Wales) situated in the heart of Llandudno, close to the beautiful mile-long Promenade and the Snowdonia National Park.

Best End Of Lamb With Basil Mousse And Turnip Gateau

Serves 4

Ingredients
4 x 4oz best end of lamb, no bone, fat or nerve (Ask the butcher to remove these)
4oz chicken mousse
4 chicken skins
½ pint veal stock
2oz turnip trimmings
1 small glass of white wine
8oz butter
1 large waxy potato
1lb turnips
Salt and pepper

For the chicken and basil mousse:
1 breast of chicken
1 egg white
¼ pint cream
1tsp fresh basil
Salt and pepper

Method

Grate the potato and turnip into a large bowl and season. Melt 1oz butter in an 8in frying pan and place the mixture of potato and turnip in the pan. Press down very tightly and put in a very hot oven at 450°F. Cook for 5 minutes, then turn and continue cooking for a further 5 minutes. When cooked, turn out and keep hot.

In a food processor, blend the chicken and egg white. When smooth, add the cream gradually, then season. Add the basil to the chicken mousse and fold in.

Season the four pieces of lamb and spread equal quantities of the chicken and basil mousse onto one side of each piece. Lay out the four chicken skins and enfold the lamb with mousse in the skins. Cut off any excess skin, tie both ends with string and also tie loosely in the centre.

Melt 2oz butter in a large pan. Place the lamb envelopes in the pan mousse-side down and seal for 1 minute. Turn the lamb and place in the oven at 375°F for 10 minutes. Remove from the pan and keep warm.

Pour off the fat and place the turnip trimmings in the pan and sweat. Deglaze with white wine and reduce until the turnips are moist. Add the veal stock and reduce again until syrupy. Strain into a clean pan, whisk in the remaining butter, season and keep hot.

Slice the lamb into 5 slices per envelope and reheat in a hot oven at 450°F. Cut the gateaux into 4 pieces and place on 4 plates. Arrange the lamb in a fan around the gateau and coat with the sauce.

The first Charity Easter 'Chick Knit' 1997 - Volunteer Workers packing 250,000 chicks with their chocolate eggs!

Gwesty Seiont Manor

Llanrug, Caernarfon LL55 2AQ
Tel: 01286 673366 Fax: 01286 672840
E-mail: www.seiontmanor@arcadianhotels.co.uk
Website: www.arcadianhotels.co.uk

When it comes to a restful weekend away, Seiont Manor has all the key ingredients ~ good food (the restaurant holds an *AA Rosette*) an impressive leisure suite with heated pool, solarium, sauna and gym and a peaceful setting next to one of the UK's most unspoilt and least heralded pieces of countryside.

The Llwyn-y-Brain restaurant gives elegant surroundings to enjoy many traditional Welsh favourites. Using the very best of local fresh products Martyn Williams produces exciting and interesting dishes for your enjoyment.

With friendly and attentive service the Seiont Manor lets you relax and enjoy yourself in first rate surroundings.

Pot Roasted Guinea Fowl
With Braised Cabbage,
Gower Potatoes And Parsnips Served
With Honey And Brecon Whisky

Serves 2

Ingredients
2½ guinea fowl (whole)
Small cabbage (Savoy) well trimmed and quartered
1lb potatoes
1lb parsnips
2 generous tblsp clear honey
8oz butter (4oz melted, 4oz diced and chilled)
2½ pints chicken stock
Mirepoix (leek trim, carrot, stock)
3 measures Brecon whisky

Method
Roast buttered guinea fowl with Mirepoix and two pints of chicken stock in oven 325°F turning constantly for approximately 1¼ to 1½ hours.

While guinea fowl is roasting, prepare vegetables.

Peel and trim potatoes and parsnips and boil together. When cooked, strain and mash, season and place into buttered Dariole moulds.

Place cabbage in a buttered pan with ½ pint chicken stock and gently braise. When cooked trim off stalks.

Sauce: After removing legs and breasts off the carcass, leave to stand (keeping the sauce warm). Place carcass and trimmings back into the roasting dish that the guinea fowl was cooked in. Add honey and whisky. Reduce to sauce consistency, constantly skimming off all the excess fat.
Strain and thicken with small dice of butter (monte). Season to taste.

Presentation: Place potato and parsnip mash at top of the plate, arrange cabbage and guinea fowl in centre. Pour the sauce around the plate and over the mash. Simply decorate with a sprig of chervil.

A tiny portion of the Velindre Voluntary Work Force enjoying their Summer 2000 get-together

Lastra Farm Hotel

AA ★★

**Amlwch, Isle of Anglesey, North Wales LL68 9TF
Tel: 01407 830906 Fax: 01407 832522**

A warm welcome awaits you at the Lastra Farm Hotel. This beautiful 17th Century farmhouse is situated ½ mile from the historic town of Amlwch and the famous Parys Mountain Copper Mine.

We are very fortunate in having locally supplied wild salmon, lobster, oysters and trout, while local butchers supply prime meat and game when in season.

We also use vegetables, herbs and fruits from neighbouring farms. From these freshest of ingredients, combined with the creative talents of our chef, come truly memorable meals.

Steak Bodafon

Ingredients
2 x 8oz sirloin
3oz grated Welsh Farmhouse Cheddar
1 leek
½ pint Bordelaise sauce (gravy)
1tsp tomato purée
½ glass port

Method
Trim the sirloin steak if required, cut a small pocket at one side.

Stuff the sirloin steak with the grated cheese and the sautéed leek.

Place sirloin steak on to a baking tray and grill on both sides to your liking.

Place the Bordelaise sauce into a thick-bottomed pan and whisk in the tomato purée. Bring to the boil.

Add the port and simmer gently, correct seasoning.

Coat the steak with the sauce.

Sprinkle with chopped parsley and serve.

SOME GOOD RECIPES FOR THOSE PEOPLE WITH FOOD INTOLERANCES

Barbara's Kitchen, PO Box 54, Pontyclun,
CF72 8WD
Tel/Fax: 01443 229304
Email enquiries@barbaraskitchen.co.uk
Website www.barbaraskitchen.co.uk

DO YOU HAVE AN INTOLERANCE TO WHEAT -
GLUTEN - DAIRY - EGG - SUGAR - YEAST?

Dream no more.

A long time ago I trained as a microwave cookery teacher and then ran a catering company in Cornwall and Hampshire. I was always being asked at every demonstration or event for a recipe for someone with a food intolerance.

Suffering from a food intolerance myself, I know from experience how hard it I to create food which is nutritional, appetising and right for your own body.

In todays world many children and adults are becoming intolerant to certain food ingredients. I can offer you RECIPES AND THE BASIC INGREDIENTS to make bread (made by hand or machine) pasta, pastry, pizza, muffins, pancakes, scones, biscuits, playdough, finger paints etc.

All the following recipes are wheat/gluten and can be dairy/egg/sugar/yeast free.

I am thrilled to be associated with the Charity Appeals Department in the publication of their first volume.

Barbara's Miracle Rolls
Wheat/Gluten/Dairy/Sugar/Yeast free
(can also be egg free)

Makes 4 large or 8-10 small
Recipe can also be used as a pizza base

Pre-heat your oven to 180° (fan assisted) - 190°C Gas 4 - 350°F. Higher temperature may be needed if using as a pizza base

Dry Ingredients
Mix gently together
1 cup white rice flour
¼ cup potato starch flour
¼ cup tapioca starch flour
1½ tsp gluten free baking powder
½ tsp crushed sea salt
1 tsp xanthan gum

Wet Ingredients
Mix together
1 large egg beaten (if no egg allowed, contact Barbara's kitchen)
2 tsp cider vinegar (if allowed)
3ozs melted butter (or 30zs allowed GFCF margarine)
1 cup warm water (may need less if using as pizza dough)

Method

Gently mix dry and wet ingredients together using a hand electric mixer. Mix should be quite 'sloppy' in texture.

To make rolls as in the photo use 4" diameter by 1" high fruit/pie tins oiled - can supply set of four.

Bake for approximately 18-20 minutes

Time may vary with your own oven. If using a muffin tray may need to decrease cooking time.

Sultanas or dried fruit can be added.

For use as a pizza base spread the dough out on a greased tin. Add herbs to dough mix if allowed.

White-Brown Loaf Recipe Using Liquid Milk©
1½ lb Loaf

Recipe available for making by hand.
Using American measuring cups/spoons.
All ingredients at room temperature.

Dry Ingredients
Gently mix together in a bowl first - except the yeast
2½ Cups white rice flour
½ Cup potato starch flour
½ Cup tapioca starch flour
1 tbsp xanthan gum
1 tsp crushed sea salt
2 tbsp sugar
1 sachet fast action dried yeast (2¼ tsp)

Wet Ingredients

3 large eggs (at room temp - beaten)
¼ cup allowed oil e.g sunflower/corn/pure virgin olive oil
1 tsp cider vinegar (optional)
½ cup soya/rice/goat/cow's milk
¾ cup hand hot water

Method

Mix all the dry ingredients together in a bowl except the yeast. Mix all the wet ingredients together and place immediately in the base of your bread machine.

Gently place the dry ingredients (except the yeast) on top of the wet ingredients, then sprinkle the yeast on top.

Use normal bake setting with a choice of light/dark crust setting.

Using a plastic spatula you may need to push down the mixture on the side of machine when it first starts mixing.

On completion of the baking time - remove tin from your machine. Remove the loaf and place on its side on a wire tray to become cold before slicing
Freezes well.

To make a brown loaf add 1tbsp treacle/molasses to wet ingredients if allowed - add pine nuts, seeds to make a granary type loaf.

Chocolate Chip Cookies
Please note any chocolate can
contain a trace of nuts

To make plain biscuits omit cocoa - chocolate. Divide mixture into 4 bowls and make selection of different flavours eg ginger, mashed banana, pure vanilla extract, allowed chocolate chips etc.

Preheat your oven to 190°C/180°C (fan assisted) 375°F Gas 5. Combine together in a bowl.

1½ cups white rice flour
¼ cup potato starch flour
¼ cup cadbury's (or allowed) cocoa powder
2 tsp xanthan gum
½ tsp gluten free baking powder
½ tsp crushed sea salt

Cream together
1¼ cups sugar
1 cup allowed GFCF soft margarine (or soft butter/margarine)

Beat together 2 medium eggs
Slowly add the beaten eggs into the sugar/ margarine mixture add:
1tsp pure vanilla extract
5oz bar of GFCF supercook belgium continental dark chocolate - grated or cut into very small pieces or GFCF Choc Chips or allowed chocolate.
I grate mine directly from the freezer.

Stir in the flour mix to the creamed sugar/margarine
Do not grease your baking tray
Place 1tsp = 40 small cookies of the mixture onto the tray
1dsp = 20 large cookies
Bake 12-15 minutes approximately - will depend upon your oven.
When cooking time has finished use a spatula to remove onto a wire tray to cool and dry.

Carrot And Pineapple/Apricot Muffins

Makes approximately 16

Using American measuring cups, muffin tray and mixing bowl paper muffin cups (optional) but as the gluten free mixture is very light the cups hold the cakes together for storage or freezing.
Preheat your oven 190°C 180°C Fan assisted 375°F Gas 4-5.

Ingredients
2½ cups white rice flour
½ cup tapioca starch flour
½ cup potato starch flour
2 cups finely grated carrot
1 cup finely crushed pineapple (small tin plus juice)
1 tsp cider vinegar (optional)
2 tsp pure vanilla extract
1 tsp xanthan gum

2tsp gluten free baking powder

½tsp - 1tsp each of gluten free mixed spice and gluten free cinnamon

2 large eggs at room temperature

1tsp bicarbonate of soda

¾ cup sugar

1 cup sunflower/corn/pure olive oil

pinch of crushed sea salt

Method

Mix the above ingredients together. The mixture should look quite 'wet' if too dry add up to ¼ cup of allowed milk or juice from soaked apricots.

Spoon into muffin cups (preferably using paper cases) or a greased muffin tray.

Bake for approximately 20 minutes until cooked when tested.

The timing will depend upon your oven. When cooked remove and cool on a wire tray.

If allowed you can use with the carrots - sultanas, choc chips, mashed banana/pear, cranberries, blueberries etc.

These muffins freeze well.

CELEBRITY RECIPES

Colin's Rice, Peas And Chicken

Donated by Colin Jackson
World, British and European Hurdles Champion

Ingredients

For the chicken:
1 x 3lb chicken (or chicken pieces)
1 onion
Tomatoes (small tin)
Garlic salt or salt, black pepper
1 red and 1 green pepper
½lb mushrooms
Soya sauce
Chicken stock cube
Sunflower oil

For rice and peas:
1lb Uncle Ben's brown rice (or long grain)
6oz red dried peas (kidney beans dried)
2-4 oz coconut cream (to taste)
Small onion (chopped)
Green or red pepper (or both)
½tsp powdered saffron

Rice and peas ~ Method

Wash and soak peas (beans) overnight. Cook for $\frac{3}{4}$-1 hour until soft. Season with salt. Add coconut cream, chopped onion and peppers. Optional: Small pieces of bacon (with rind cut off) can be added for extra flavour. Boil together for 5 minutes until coconut cream has dissolved and onion and peppers cooked. Add rice, bring to boil.

Chicken ~ Method
Cut chicken in portions, slice onion and add to chicken with salt, pepper and soya sauce. Marinade for minimum 2 hours. Remove each piece from marinade sauce. In frying pan with oil, brown each piece both sides. Remove and place all pieces (in large saucepan) with marinade, onion and sauce. Add small tin of tomatoes and mushrooms. Mix chicken stock, add to saucepan. Cook slowly for $\frac{1}{2}$-$\frac{3}{4}$ hour. Add more salt or black pepper or soya according to taste. Thicken with McDougal's granules. Serve on bed of rice and peas.

Members of the Queen's Dragoon Guards (the Welsh Cavalry) prior to their marathon charity cycle ride from North Germany to Newport!

David's Beef Wellington

Donated by David Gower
Former England and Hampshire County Cricket Club

Ingredients
3lbs beef fillet
¼lb paté
½lb finely chopped mushrooms
1lb puff pastry (or shortcrust)
Beaten egg to glaze
Salt, pepper
1tblsp oil

Method
Preheat oven to 230°C (425°F)

Rub the beef with salt, pepper and oil. Roast on a rack for 40 minutes. Remove and leave to cool.

When cool, cover the top and sides with the paté and chopped mushrooms.

Roll out the pastry to ¼in thickness ~ large enough to envelope the meat. Put the fillet top side down on the pastry and enclose into a parcel sealing the ends.

Turn meat seam side down and decorate with spare pastry if you can be bothered!

Glaze with the beaten egg.

Bake for a further 40 minutes or so, till the pastry is golden brown and puffed up.

Note: Tastes even better if served with a red wine sauce.

Salmon a la Botham

Donated by Ian Botham
Former England and Durham County Cricketer

Ingredients
1 freshly caught salmon (approximately 5lbs weight) cleaned and inners removed
Freshly squeezed lemon juice
2oz butter
Salt and freshly ground black pepper
Parsley and lemon wedges to decorate

Method
Place fish on a large piece of kitchen foil. Dot inside and out with butter.
Pour lemon juice over the flesh of the fish.
Season the inside.
Wrap in foil, not too tightly, to make a parcel.
Place in roasting tin (for appearance it is better to have head and tail on fish, however these can be removed beforehand if wished).
Place in oven for approximately 45 minutes.
Remove and decorate with lemon wedges and parsley.

Note: Serve with new potatoes (skins not removed), green salad with garlic dressing. Serve with a chilled dry white wine.

Myra's Stuffed Aubergines

Donated by Sir Harry Secombe
Radio/TV Celebrity

Serves 8

Ingredients
2lbs lean minced beef
8oz chopped onions
Clove of garlic
Mixed herbs
½ pint tomato juice
Dash of Worcester sauce
3tsps Bovril
Black pepper
8 aubergines
Breadcrumbs

Method
Put minced beef in a heavy-based saucepan, cover with water and bring to the boil for 5 minutes.

Pour off liquid, then add onions, crushed garlic, herbs and tomato juice. Mix Bovril and Worcester sauce with a little hot water and add to the mince.

Simmer for 45 minutes or until tender.

Place aubergines in water and simmer until the skins start to wrinkle (do not overcook). Cut in half and scoop out flesh and mix with the minced beef. Fill the aubergine shells with the mixture and bake in a moderate oven for 30 minutes.

Cover with fine breadcrumbs and place under the grill to brown. Serve at once.

Chicken And Asparagus Casserole

Donated by Terry Wogan
Radio/TV Presenter

Ingredients
6 chicken breasts
1 large tin green asparagus spears
2tblsp medium sherry
Paprika pepper
1 tin condensed mushroom soup
½ pint double cream
4 heaped tblsp grated Cheddar cheese

Method
Gently poach chicken breasts in a little chicken stock for approximately 15 minutes.

Grease a shallow casserole dish that will take the chicken breasts in one layer.

Place the drained asparagus on the bottom of the greased casserole dish.

Place chicken breasts on top. Combine soup, cream and sherry in a saucepan and heat gently stirring constantly.

Pour over chicken and asparagus. Sprinkle over the grated cheese and paprika and season to taste.

Bake in a hot oven 400°F for 20 minutes.

Tom Jones' Brandy Snaps

Donated by Tom Jones
Singer

Makes about 3 dozen

Ingredients
1 cup lightly packed light brown sugar
one third of a cup of dark Karo syrup
1 stick sweet butter (4oz)
1 cup plus 3tblsp sifted flour
1tblsp brandy

Filling
1 cup double cream
2tblsp sugar
1tsp brandy

Method
In a saucepan melt butter, sugar and syrup together over medium-low heat, stirring with a wooden spoon. Bring to beginning to boil and remove from heat.

Stir in flour and ginger until smooth. Add in brandy. Drop 4 half-teaspoonsful on a greased cookie sheet.

Bake, watching closely, at 350°F until golden brown, but not dark.

While these are baking, repeat with a second cookie sheet. When you remove first batch from oven, pop second batch in. Repeat until all batter is used.

Allow cookies to cool 30-60 seconds. Working quickly with a spatula, shape the cookies into a horn-of-plenty shape.

To make filling, whip cream until still. Add sugar and brandy and beat for a few seconds. Do not fill shells more than ½ hour before serving.

You can also serve the shells and cream separately.

**Members of the 'Halifax Building Society'
(Newport and Cardiff Branches)
fund-raising at Cardiff Bay.**

Bara Brith

Donated by Sir Anthony Hopkins
Actor

Ingredients
1lb self-raising flour
1lb mixed dried fruit
2tblsp warm marmalade
1 egg (beaten)
6oz brown sugar
½ pint warm strained tea
1tsp mixed spice

Method
Place the fruit and sugar in a mixing bowl and soak overnight in the strained tea.

Sieve the flour and mixed spice and warm the marmalade.

Add the flour, warm marmalade and beaten egg to the soaked fruit. Mix well.

Pour the mixture into a greased loaf tin.

Bake for 1½ hours on Gas Mark 4 (180°C/350°F).

Cool on a wire rack.

Serve sliced and buttered.

Orange Raisin Loaf
Donated by Julie Smith MBE
Appeals Officer Velindre Hospital Charity

Ingredients

9oz self-raising flour
1 level tsp mixed spice
½ level tsp cinnamon
Pinch of salt
3oz margarine
4oz soft brown sugar
6oz raisins
1 medium-sized orange
2tblsp golden syrup
½ pint milk
1 large egg

Method

Preheat oven to 325°F (Gas Mark 3)

Grease a 2lb loaf tin (9in x 5in) and line the base.

Rub in margarine and stir in sugar and raisins.

Grate the rind from the orange and add to mixture.

Beat 1tblsp syrup with egg and milk and add flour, mixing well.

Turn into the tin and smooth the top.

Bake in the centre of the pre-heated oven for approximately 1 hour or until firm and golden.

Top can be decorated with orange slices and remaining tblsp of syrup brushed over slices.

Julie

Easter 'Chick Knit' stuffing crew at a SWALEC
Charity Chocolate 'Stuff-a-thon'! Together with
the workers are Appeal Patrons Stan Stennett
(centre) and Roy Noble (middle right)

Moist Boiled Fruit Cake
Donated by Roy Noble
BBC Radio and TV Wales and
Velindre Appeal Patron

Ingredients
8oz margarine
6oz sugar
½ pint milk
1lb mixed fruit
1lb flour
1 heaped tsp bicarbonate of soda
2tsp mixed spice
2tsp vanilla essence
2 eggs

Method
Place margarine in saucepan with sugar over a low heat until sugar has melted.

Add ½ pint milk and 1lb mixed fruit and bring to boil.

Boil for two minutes, stirring continuously.

Remove from heat and quickly stir in flour, bicarb and spice.

Add beaten eggs and vanilla essence. (Add sherry if desired).

Place into an 8in cake tin and cook at 150°C for 1 hour.

Leave in tin for 10 minutes before removing.

Note: To make this into a celebration cake add 2tblsp of sherry.

Nick's Banana Raisin Ring

Donated by Nick Faldo
Champion Golfer

Ingredients
4oz butter or margarine
6oz Castor sugar
2 eggs
3 bananas
½ cup chopped raisins
½ level tsp bicarbonate of soda
1tblsp milk
1tsp vanilla essence
6oz self-raising flour

Method
Cream butter and sugar.
Add eggs one at a ime, beating well after each addition.
Stir in mashed banana and raisins.
Dissolve bicarbonate of soda in milk and vanilla essence.
Add alternately with sifted flour to egg mixture. Stir well.
Place in a well-greased and floured 8in ring tin.
Bake in centre of moderate gas oven (350°F/180°C) for 30-40 minutes.
When cold, ice with lemon water icing.

Note: Keeps fresh and moist for a long time.

Apple And Rhubarb Almond Sponge

Donated by Richard Branson
Chairman, Virgin Group

Ingredients
1lb cooking apples
1lb rhubarb
Grated rind and juice of 1 orange
3oz demerara sugar
2oz sultanas

For the sponge:
3oz butter
3oz sugar
2 eggs
A few drops almond essence
3oz self-raising flour
1oz ground almonds
Salt
A little milk

Method
Peel and slice apples.
Wash and cut rhubarb into 1in pieces.
Put in a saucepan with orange juice and rind, sugar and sultanas.
Simmer for about 15 minutes.
Pour into greased ovenproof dish.
Cream butter and sugar.
Add eggs and almond essence.
Mix in flour, ground almonds and salt.

Add a little milk to make a dropping consistency.
Then spoon over the fruit and sprinkle the top with
flaked almonds.
Cook at 180°C (Gas Mark 4) for 35-40 minutes.
Serve hot with custard or cream.

**Anne Thomas (left) - Velindre Hospital regular
fund-raiser, presenting one of her many cheque's
to her favourite 'Princess Margaret Ward'.**

Stuffed Tomatoes

Donated by John Burnett
**Appeals Co-ordinator,
Velindre Hospital/Charity**

Serves 8 people

Ingredients
8 large tomatoes
¾oz best margarine
¾oz plain flour
¼ pint milk
1oz Cheddar cheese
2oz chopped ham
1 tsp made mustard
Parsley to garnish

Method
Cut tops off tomatoes at about ¼ of the way down and scoop out the centre pulp.
Melt the margarine in a saucepan. Stir in the flour. Stir over a low heat for ½ a minute.
Add the milk slowly and continue to stir over heat until the mixture is thick and creamy.
Add the cheese, mustard and ham. Remove from heat and cool.
When cold place the mixture into the tomatoes. Replace the tops and garnish with parsley.

Note: To achieve an attractive effect, the tomato tops may be cut in 'starfish' shapes with a very sharp, pointed knife.

John Burnett.

**John Burnett (Charity Manager) receiving
one of many donations from the staff of the
Alliance and Leicester Buliding Society, Cardiff**

Spinach Bake

Donated by Carolyn Smith
Appeals Officer
Velindre Hospital

Serves 4

Ingredients

½ bag frozen spinach (thawed)
1 tub cottage cheese
¼ lb grated cheddar cheese
1 finely chopped onion
4 tbsp flour (wholemeal if preferred)
4 eggs
2 sliced tomatoes

Method

Combine all the ingredients together, adding extra flour if consistency seems a little runny! (If desired before putting in the oven add a little grated cheese over the top to brown.) Bake in the oven at 180°C for ½ hour, add the sliced tomato to the top and bake for a further 15mins or until risen and cooked inside.

Bon Appetit!

Carolyn

Country Plum Pudding

Donated by Owen Money
BBC Radio and TV Wales

Ingredients
Suet crust pastry:
½lb flour
4oz suet
1tsp baking powder
Cold water to mix

Filling:
1lb yellow egg plums or Victoria plums
4oz sugar

Method
Sieve the flour and baking powder together, mix in suet.
Add enough cold water to make a pastry dough.
Cut off a ¼ of the mixture and retain.
Roll out the remainder onto a surface and cut into a circle about twice the size of the top of the pudding basin. Lift very carefully and ease in to line the basin.
Halve and de-stone the plums and layer with the sugar in the basin. Trim the pastry around the top of the basin.
Add the trimmings to the retained quarter and roll out to fit the top of the pudding. Dampen the edges, place the pastry lid on top and seal the edges.

Cover with greaseproof paper and steam for approximately 1½ hours.

Note: Serve very hot with custard or cream.

Stan Stennett's Lemon Cake

Donated by Stan Stennett
Radio/TV Celebrity/Velindre Appeal Patron

Ingredients
4oz margarine
6oz Castor sugar
6oz self-raising flour
4tblsp milk
2 large eggs
Grated rind of one lemon

Method
Mix all the ingredients together in a mixer.
Line and grease a 2lb loaf tin.
Cook at 350°F (180°C/Gas Mark 4) for 45 minutes until firm.
Leave cake in tin.
In a saucepan, heat 3tblsp of icing sugar and 3tblsp of lemon juice.
Make holes on top of cake with metal skewer or knitting needle and spoon or pour lemon juice and sugar over the top, whilst hot.
Important ~ leave cake in tin until cold.

Note: This cake freezes well. If you freeze, leave paper on cake.

Stan Stennett (Charity Appeal Patron) showing soldiers of the Queen's Dragoon Guards around the hospital

Alicia's Crunchy Peach Crumble

Donated by Jimmy Young
Radio Presenter

Serves 6

Ingredients
6oz (175g) plain flour
3oz (75g) butter (chilled and diced)
3oz (75g) demerara sugar
½tsp salt
4 fresh peaches, skinned and sliced
or 822g tin of sliced peaches, drained

Method
Mix the flour and salt together in a bowl.
Add the butter and rub in lightly using your fingertips until the mixture resembles fine breadcrumbs. Add the sugar and mix well.
Put the peaches in a medium-sized shallow ovenproof dish and spread out evenly.
Cover the peaches with the crumble mixture.
Cook in a preheated oven Gas Mark 6 or 200°C/400°F for 25 minutes or until golden brown.
Serve warm with whipped cream, ice-cream or custard.

Note: If you want the crumble to be less crunchy, put the demerara sugar in a blender for few seconds or use Castor sugar instead. You can, of course, use fruits other than peaches, such as nectarines, apples, blackberries, apricots etc.

Emlyn's Summer Sole Fillets

Donated by Emlyn Hughes
Former Liverpool and England Football Captain

Serves 4

Ingredients
4 x 175g (6oz) lemon sole or plaice, fresh or defrosted, skinned
15ml (1 tablespoon) lemon juice
45ml (3 tablespoons) water or dry white wine
2 tomatoes, roughly chopped
2 spring onions, chopped
5ml (1 teaspoon) seafood seasoning

Method
Fold the fish fillets in half, place in a large shallow pan.
Pour over the lemon juice and water or wine.
Mix together the tomatoes and spring onions, spoon over the fish fillets.
Sprinkle with seafood seasoning, cover and cook on a low heat for 10-15 minutes.
Serve with new potatoes, carrots and courgettes.

Note: A delicious recipe the whole year round, ask the fishmonger for advice on which fish to buy and to fillet and skin the fish if necessary.

Hilary's Grandmothers' Recipe For Chopped Liver

Donated by Esther Rantzen
Television Presenter

Ingredients
2lbs chicken liver (calves liver may be used)
1 large Spanish onion
3-4 hard-boiled eggs
1tblsp melted chicken fat (optional)
Oil for frying onions and liver
Salt and pepper to taste

Method
Fry the sliced onion in a little oil until golden (for about 10 minutes).

Remove from the pan. Chop in food processor for about 1 minute until very finely chopped. Place in a bowl.

Fry the livers until well done (about 10 minutes). Chop in a food processor until smooth. Add to the onions.

Reserve one egg yolk for garnish. Finely chop hard boiled eggs in food processor. Add to liver and onions and mix to smooth paté. If it is not moist enough a little of the pan juices may be added or about 1 tablespoon of chicken fat.

Season to taste with salt and pepper. Garnish with chopped egg yolk.

Esther Rantzen

Woosie's Shepherd's Pie

Donated by Ian Woosnam
Champion Golfer

Serves 4-6

Ingredients
2 finely chopped onions
4-6 diced carrots
3oz unsalted butter
1lb cooked minced beef
6fl oz beef stock or gravy
1 level tblsp tomato ketchup
¼tsp Worcester sauce
Salt and black pepper
2-3tblsp milk
1lb mashed potatoes

Method
Cook the onions in 1oz of the butter until soft, add the meat and carrots and cook until lightly brown.
Stir in the stock, ketchup and Worcester sauce, season. Beat the remaining melted butter and the milk into the potatoes. Put the meat in a greased ovenproof dish, cover with potato and ripple the top with a fork. Bake near the top of the oven heated to 420°F or Gas Mark 7 for 30 minutes or until golden brown. Serve the pie hot, on its own or with green vegetables.

'After a hard day on the golf course, I love to come home to my favourite meal of Shepherd's Pie.'

Gary's Paella

Donated by Gary Lineker
Television Presenter and former
England Soccer Star

Ingredients
2tblsp oil
1 onion peeled and chopped
3 chicken joints ~ halved
8oz squid rings
1lb rice
½tsp powdered saffron
Salt and pepper
1tsp paprika
2tblsp tomato purée
1tblsp fresh parsley
½ pint chicken stock
juice of half a lemon
1lb mussels ~ frozen on the half shell and defrosted
4oz cockles ~ frozen, shelled
4oz whole prawns

Method
Heat oil in a large frying pan and cook onion and garlic until soft.
Add chicken pieces and cook for 5 minutes.
Add squid rings and cook for 2 minutes turning everything over.
Add rice and stir.

Add saffron, paprika, tomato purée and parsley, then add stock and lemon juice.
Bring to boil, then turn down to simmer.
Add mussels and cockles and cook for 20 minutes ~ or until rice is tender.
Ten minutes before end of cooking time add prawns.

Early arrivals following the first 'Cancer Research Wales' (Velindre) Tour de Cardiff Family Bike Ride - 1994

Spaghetti Alla Carbonara

Donated by Nigel Walker

Former Welsh Rugby International and Radio/TV Commentator

Ingredients

10oz pancetta or rindless bacon (diced)
1¼lb spaghetti
6tblsp grated pecorino cheese
6 egg yolks
Salt and freshly ground pepper
3tblsp freshly grated parmesan cheese
1 hot red chilli pepper

Method

Combine the pancetta (or bacon) and chilli pepper in a skillet until some of the fat has melted. Increase the heat and cook until the pancetta (or bacon) browns.

Bring a large pot of salted water to boil and cook the spaghetti in it until al dente. Drain, reserving ½ cup water. Transfer to a serving dish.

Mix the pecorino with the reserved spaghetti cooking water. Mix in the egg yolks with a fork, then add a little salt and pepper. Tip the contents of the skillet over the spaghetti. Add the egg mixture and toss well.

Note: Sprinkle with parmesan cheese.

Cawl Cynyn

Donated by Ieuan Evans
Former Welsh Rugby International and Sports Commentator

Ingredients
2lb Welsh neck of lamb
2lb potatoes
1lb carrots
1 onion
1 small swede
1 small turnip
1 parsnip
5 sprigs of parsley
1 leek
Salt and pepper

Method
Remove as much fat as possible from lamb and place in a saucepan, cover with water and bring to the boil.
Skim any residue of fat from top of water.
Add all diced vegetables (except parsley), water and season to taste.
Simmer for 3-3½ hours. Serve hot, decorated with sprigs of parsley.
Note: I like to remove potatoes into a small side dish and mash them when eating this delicious cawl.

Spicy Tomato Sauce

Donated by Gary Rhodes
**A recipe taken from *'Rhodes Around Britain'*
TV Series**

Makes about 450g (1lb)

Ingredients
85ml (3fl oz) olive oil
3 shallots or 2 onions, finely chopped
2 garlic cloves, crushed
A few fresh basil, thyme and tarragon leaves
900g (2lb) tomatoes, skinned and seeded
2tblsp red wine vinegar
1tsp Castor sugar
Salt and freshly ground white pepper
2-3 drops Tabasco sauce

Method
Warm the olive oil in a pan and add the chopped shallots or onions, the garlic and the herbs. It's best to have the herbs in sprigs, as these can then be easily removed at the end of cooking.

Allow the shallots and herbs to cook for 4-5 minutes until tender.

Cut the tomato flesh into 5mm (¼in) dice and add to the shallots. Have the pan on a very low heat, just on a light simmer, and cook for about 45 minutes. The sauce may cook a little quicker, or take a little longer ~ this will really depend on the water content of the tomatoes.

After 45 minutes, add the wine vinegar and sugar and cook for a further 15 minutes. The tomatoes should have taken on an almost lumpy sauce texture; if the sauce is very thick, simply fold in a little more olive oil.

Allow to cool until just warm then season with salt, pepper and Tabasco. The sauce is now ready.

Note: This sauce goes well with seafood of all types. It's almost like eating a loose spicy tomato chutney. Once made, it can be kept chilled for up to two weeks.

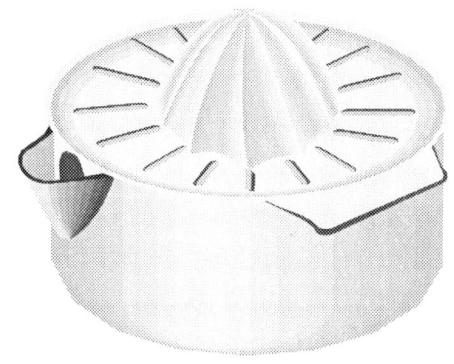